THE PYTHON PROGRAMMER'S SURVIVAL GUIDE

How to Make It Through Coding Without
Losing Your Mind, Your Hair or Your Will to Live

Written by

Matt Jordan

THE PYTHON PROGRAMMER'S SURVIVAL GUIDE

© 2025 Matt Jordan

This book is a work of nonfiction with comedic elements. While programming concepts are referenced, the tone is intentionally humorous.

Published by ZeroToPyHero Publishing

www.zerotopyhero.com

To every Python programmer who has ever whispered 'why' at their screen.
You're among friends.

Table of Contents

INTRODUCTION

So You Chose Python... Bold Move

Welcome, brave soul.

If you're reading this, it means one of three things has happened:

1. You recently decided to learn Python and you're already questioning your life choices.

2. You've been a Python developer for years and you're now emotionally numb, spiritually drained, and looking for a book that understands your pain.

3. Someone gave you this as a "fun little gift," and now you're wondering if it was meant as a warning.

Whatever brought you here, you're in the right place. If you believe in destiny, destiny brought you to this book. If you believe in karma, you are either being rewarded or punished with this book.

This is not a tutorial.
This is not a course.
This is not the place to learn what a variable is, unless you're into that sort of thing.

No.

This is a survival guide. A book for anyone who has ever tried to make Python do something simple and somehow ended up with:

- five errors
- a mysterious indentation problem
- three different versions of Python on their machine
- and a spiritual headache

Python is marketed as "easy to learn."
Yes, in the same way IKEA furniture is "easy to assemble."

Sure, the pieces fit together.
Sure, the instructions look friendly.
But if you're not careful, you'll blink, and suddenly you've:

- created a recursion monster
- corrupted your virtual environment
- broken pip
- and summoned an error message so long it requires its own table of contents

But don't worry, Python also has its beautiful moments.
The moments when the code runs perfectly.
The moments when everything just clicks.
The moments when you feel like a wizard whispering to the machine and the machine actually listens.

Those moments are rare.
Treasure them.

The rest of the time, you're going to need:

- patience
- humor
- a sense of perspective
- emotional support snacks
- and, apparently, this book

I wrote this guide for the entire Python tribe:

- the beginner who still thinks print() is a personality trait
- the intermediate developer who has seen stuff
- the senior developer who now communicates exclusively in StackOverflow links
- and the hobbyist who updates Python once every presidential election (or when a new monarch takes the throne, if you are from those parts of the world) and hopes nothing breaks

This book is for all of you.

Because despite our differences, Python programmers share a universal truth:

We are all suffering, just at different skill levels.

Beginners fear semicolons.
Veterans fear async.
Everyone fears pip.

You are not alone.

In the chapters ahead, we'll explore:

- the emotional journey of debugging
- the horror of indentation
- the chaos of virtual environments
- the questionable life choices surrounding decorators
- and the moment you realize "works on my machine" is not, in fact, a valid excuse

We'll laugh together.
We'll cry together.
We'll Google together.

You'll recognize yourself in these pages.

You'll probably deny it.

You'll definitely screenshot parts and send them to friends with the caption "this is too real."

And somewhere between the jokes, the sarcasm, and the shared trauma, you might even find a little comfort; a reminder that coding is messy because humans are messy, and Python, no matter how elegant it tries to be, is also written by humans.

So take a deep breath.
Refill your coffee.
Save your file (seriously, save it).
And step boldly into the Pythonverse.

You've survived this far.

Let's keep going together.

Welcome to The Python Programmer's Survival Guide.

You're going to make it.
Probably.

Matt Jordan

Part 1
The Beginner Years: Hope, Confusion, and print()

CHAPTER 1
Installing Python: The First Boss Fight

Let's start with a universal truth: nobody installs Python correctly the first time. Nobody.
Not beginners. Not professionals. Not the people who wrote Python. I'm convinced that even Guido van Rossum wakes up some mornings wondering why his PATH variable is angry again.

Installing Python is supposed to be step one.
A formality.
A warm-up.

Instead, it becomes your first lesson in "computers do not care how optimistic you are."

The Beginner Expectation

You picture yourself downloading Python, double-clicking the installer, watching a friendly little progress bar glide across the screen, and then triumphantly typing python into your terminal as angels sing in the background.

The Reality

You download Python.

You run the installer.

You open your terminal and type:

...and your computer answers:

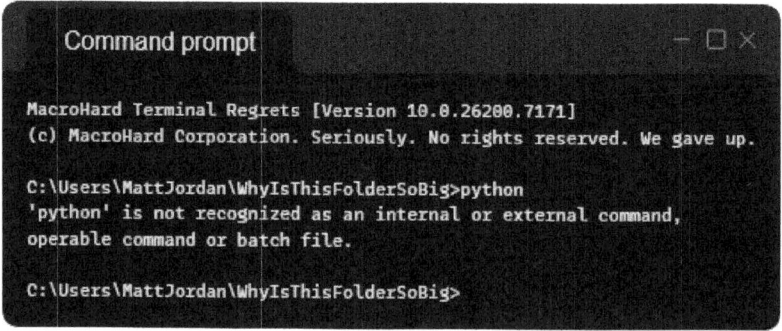

In that moment, something inside you wilts.
Not your hope, because that disappeared two steps ago, no, this is deeper. This is your soul quietly exiting through your shoes.

The Windows Checkbox of Destiny

If you're on Windows, the installer asks you a seemingly harmless question:

Add Python to PATH?

It should be checked by default, right?
Of course not. Python treats this checkbox like a trapdoor to test your reflexes.
Veterans hit it so fast they leave fingerprints in the glass.

Beginners miss it and spend three days wondering if Python is a myth.

python vs python3: Choose Your Fighter

On macOS and Linux, things get even more philosophical.

You type:

and the system gives you:

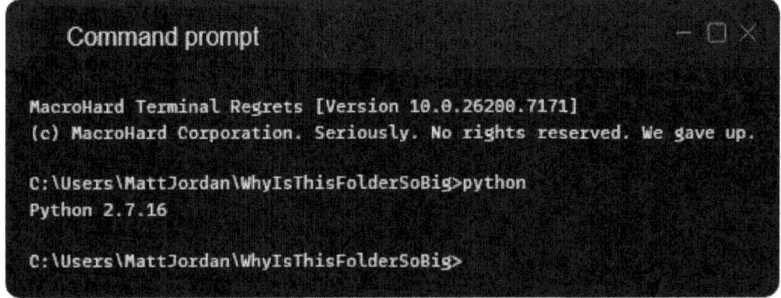

Python 2.
A version so old its documentation might as well be in a museum.

So you try:

And you get:

Much better.
Except now you get to enjoy a decade-long identity crisis where nobody tells you which one you're supposed to use. Every tutorial online chooses a different side, like parents arguing during a family trip.

pip vs pip3: The Sequel Nobody Asked For

You finally get Python running. Great.

Then you try installing a package:

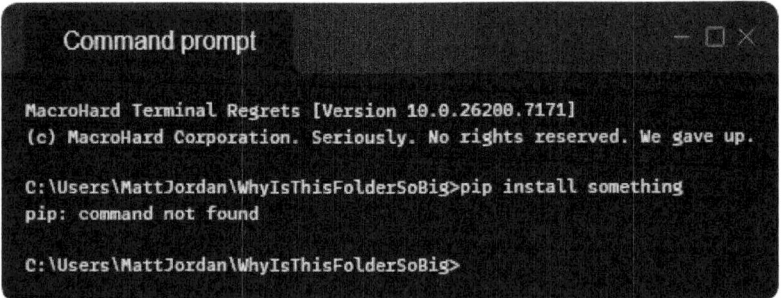

And your computer responds with the smug confidence of a machine that knows exactly how much power it has over your happiness:

So you try:

And now it works.

Congratulations.
You have officially entered **The Great Python / Python3 / pip / pip3 Quadrant of Mystical Nonsense.**
No map.
No guide.
Only suffering.

The PATH Labyrinth

Setting PATH manually is one of the most delicate operations in computing. One wrong character and suddenly your system behaves like it's had a small stroke.

New developers copy instructions from StackOverflow like they're ancient spells:

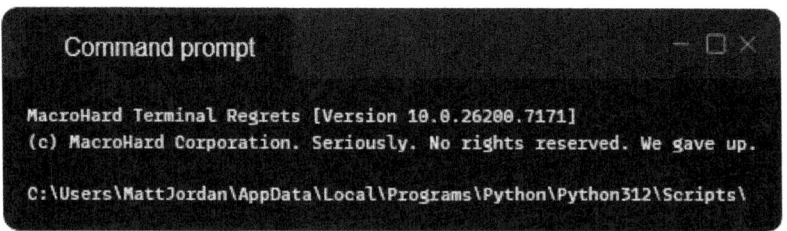

A long path. A cursed path. A path that, if typed wrong, will send you into an identity crisis about who you are and why you chose programming when carpentry was right there.

"Which Python Is Running?" The Existential Question

At some point, every developer reaches this moment:

You run your script.
It errors.
You fix the error.
It still errors.

Then you realize the horrifying truth:

You edited the wrong version of Python.

You have:

- Python from the Microsoft Store

- Python from python.org
- Python installed by some app
- Python installed by some other app
- Python installed by your package manager
- Python that came with something you installed in 2016 and forgot about and another version you installed when Covid hit because you now had all the time in the world

Your laptop is basically a Python refugee camp.

The Joy of Finally Running Your First Command

But eventually, after the battles, the mistakes, the false starts, the spiritual crisis, you type:

python3

or maybe

python

and you see:

>>>

The little triple arrow of hope.

You've done it.

You've installed Python.

You've beaten the first boss fight.

You are now officially a Python programmer, because you've already experienced your first moment of "why is this so complicated?"

And that, my friend, is the true beginning of your journey.

CHAPTER 2
Your First print(): The Last Time Things Felt Easy

Your first print() is the last peaceful moment of your Python journey.
It's pure.
It's simple.
It works.
Python smiles at you like, "See? I'm friendly."
And you believe it which is adorable in hindsight.

Everything after this moment is a slow slide into emotional complexity, but for now...
you're untouchable.

The First Time You Type It

You open your editor, crack your knuckles like a hero preparing for greatness, and write:

```
main.py

print("Hello, World!")
```

You press run.

It works.

It just... works.

Python looks at you with warm eyes and says, "See? I'm a simple and elegant language. You and I are going to get along great."

You believe it.

This is how abusive relationships start.

A Taste of Power

That first output in the console hits you like caffeine straight to the soul.

The computer obeyed you.
You typed rituals into the void and the void answered politely.
You feel clever.
You feel capable.
You feel powerful.
You start wondering why everyone says programming is hard.

"I mean, come on. This is easy."

Spoiler:
It is not easy.
You're just standing in the doorway of the house, admiring the paint, not realizing the basement contains a nest of recursive spiders.

But let's allow you this moment.

The Chapter Where Python Pretends to Be Your Friend

print() is Python's charming front porch.
It holds the door open, smiles warmly, and says:

"Come on in. No trouble here."

Later, Python will forget this promise.

Later, you will discover:

- indentation that ruins lives
- errors that lecture you like a disappointed parent
- environments that corrupt themselves at 3 in the morning
- and the word "async," which should come with a health and safety warning

But for now, it's all sunshine and function calls.

Where Beginners Live for Months

Beginners use print() like it's duct tape.

Debugging? print()
Confusion? print()
Existential crisis? print() with an emoji they don't realize won't render properly.

There is no judgment here.
Even veteran developers secretly return to print() like comfort food.

We call it print-based debugging.
Others call it "unprofessional."
Those people have cold mechanical hearts and cannot be trusted.

Real developers know:

```
print("Why isn't this working?")
```

is the truest poetry in the Python language.

Veterans Remember the Innocence

Ask an experienced Pythonista about their first print and watch their face soften.
For a moment, they're transported back to a simpler time, before they knew what circular imports were, or why pip sometimes behaves like a dragon with a toothache.

They remember the joy.
The clarity.
The optimism.

They remember thinking, "Python is so clean and readable!"
They did not yet know that readable code can still confuse you at 2 AM while you wonder who wrote it and then slowly realize... it was you.

The Turning Point

After enough print() victories, beginners start experimenting.

Variables? print them.
Loops? print inside them.
Functions? print from within every branch just to make sure they're doing anything at all.

Eventually, the beginner proudly announces:

"I think I understand Python!"

And Python, sitting silently in the corner, whispers:

"Soon."

Because the moment they step beyond print(), the training wheels come off and the language reveals its true personality.

Not cruel.
Not hostile.
Just... mischievous.

But For Now, Celebrate This Win

print() is the one line of code that always feels comforting. Even years later, when you're knee-deep in async, decorators, and the emotional ruins of a package conflict, print() is the lighthouse reminding you of where you started.

It's the last time everything felt straightforward.

The last moment before the hero's journey begins.

So take a breath.
Enjoy the simplicity while it lasts.

Python's about to get interesting.

CHAPTER 3
Variables: Where Beginners Choose Cute Names and Veterans Choose Chaos

Variables are supposed to be simple.
They're just boxes where you store stuff.
Beginners hear this and think, "Easy. I can do that."

Veterans hear this and laugh the long, weary laugh of someone who has found a variable named data_final_FINAL_really_final3 in a production system.

Beginners Start Out Wholesome

Beginners treat variable names like pets. They pick them with love.

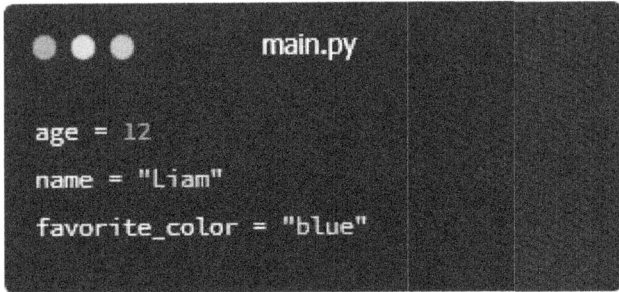

```
● ● ●                main.py

age = 12
name = "Liam"
favorite_color = "blue"
```

These names have personality.
They have charm.
They suggest that the beginner is still a hopeful person who has not yet fought in the naming trenches in the Pythonian Wars.

Beginners choose names like pets:
fluffy, cookie, dragonEgg.

They're proud of them.
Veterans? Veterans choose names that look like regrets in code form:

temp, x, data_final_FINAL.py.

Veterans Choose Violence

Somewhere along the way, something inside a developer breaks.

Naming things becomes hard.
Too hard.
So they give up.

You start finding code like:

And the developer who wrote this says, "It's self-explanatory."

No, it's not.
This is a math puzzle someone left behind in a cave.

Then there are the real gems:

```
● ● ●                main.py

tmp = something()
tmp2 = do_more(tmp)
result = do_more(tmp2)
```

A trilogy with no emotional payoff.

And let's not forget the classics:

```
● ● ●                main.py

config = config2
data = new_data
data2 = data3
```

This is not programming.
This is a cry for help.

The Naming Crisis Hits Everyone

There comes a moment, usually around 2 AM, when you're
staring at a variable thinking:

"What do I even call you?"

This simple question can burn an entire hour of your life.
You try things like:

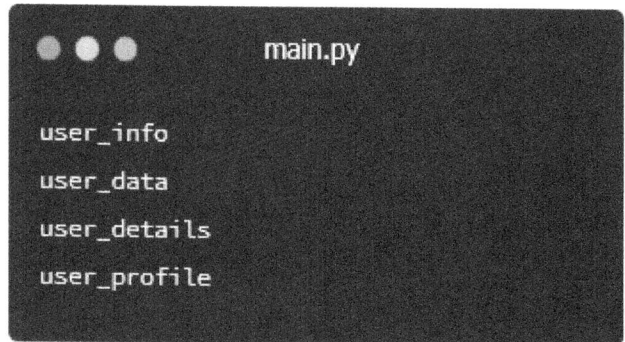

```
●  ●  ●              main.py

user_info
user_data
user_details
user_profile
```

And that's when the fear sets in.

They all look correct.
They all look wrong.
You're not even sure what "user" means anymore.

If naming things feels like a small existential crisis, you're doing it right.

The Comfort of Renaming

Python gives you many tools.
One of the most important, though rarely mentioned, is the ability to rename things six times before you're satisfied.

You tell yourself:

"I'll clean this up later."

You won't.
But the lie is part of the workflow.

Variable Names Reveal a Developer's Soul

If you ever want to understand a programmer on a deep emotional level, don't look at their LinkedIn profile. Look at their variable names.

Optimists write:

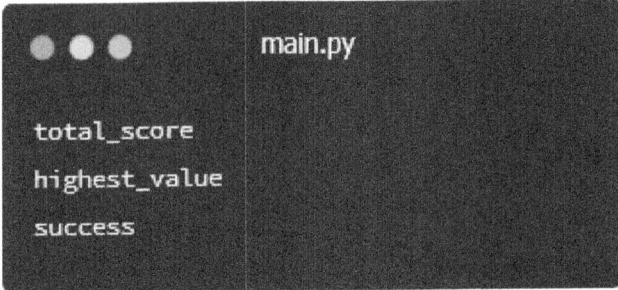

Realists write:

Developers who have given up on humanity write:

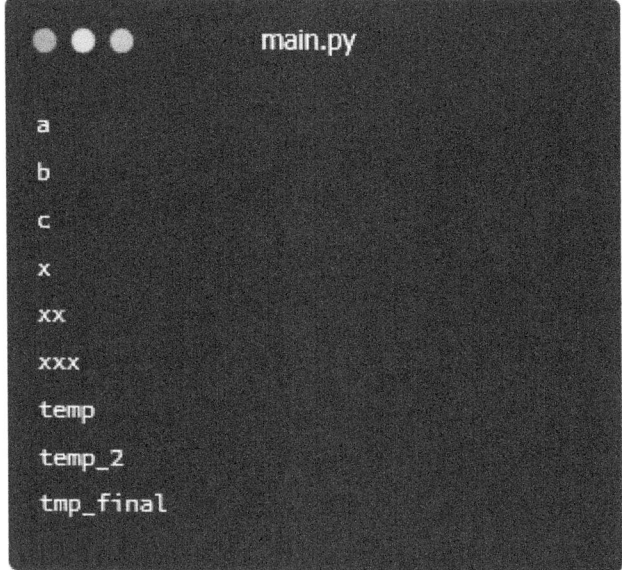

And then there are the true veterans, those ancient coders who have stared too long into the abyss. Their code contains names like:

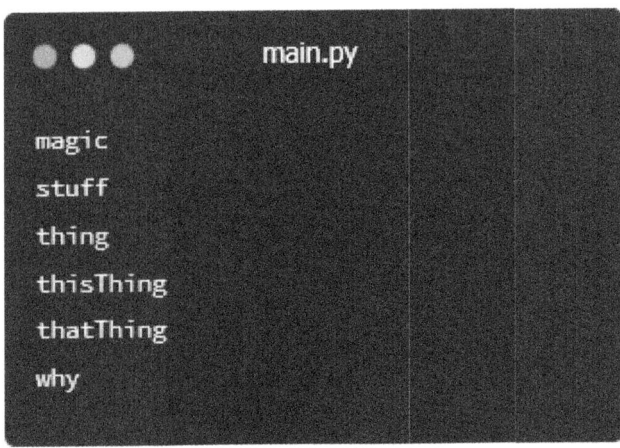

```
● ● ●              main.py

magic
stuff
thing
thisThing
thatThing
why
```

If you ever see a variable named "why", back away slowly. The developer was not okay.

The Great Naming Lie

You will hear a maxim in programming:

"Good code is self-documenting."

This is adorable.
Like believing unicorns pay taxes.

The truth is that every developer, at every skill level, has a naming graveyard hidden deep in their repository. Entire generations of failed names. Histories of confusion, panic, and regret.

But Here's the Secret

Even though naming variables is hard, you will get better at it.
Not perfect.
Not consistent.
Just... better.

You'll start to understand what "good enough" looks like.
You'll learn that readable beats clever.
And you'll begin to recognize the warning signs of a variable name that's about to cause future-you emotional damage.

Naming things is not a test.
It's a journey.
One all Pythonistas take.

So don't stress.

Everyone struggles with this.
Everyone overthinks it.
Everyone makes a mess.

You're in great company.

Now take a sip of coffee and get ready, because the next chapter introduces the thing that unites all developers across all languages, all levels, all time zones:

Errors.

CHAPTER 4
Errors: Python's Sweet, Sweet Punishment

There's nothing quite like the moment you run your code, sit back with confidence, and then watch your terminal explode into a wall of red text that looks like Python is yelling at you in several dialects at once.

This is the chapter where innocence dies.

Errors Are Not Mistakes

Let's get one thing straight before we dive in.

Errors aren't failures, they're Python's love language.
Some languages whisper warnings.
Python throws a brick with notes attached.

Think of errors as little emotional notes from the interpreter:

- "You forgot something."
- "You misunderstood something."
- "You tried something bold, and I respect that, but no."
- "You're not ready for this feature, young Padawan."

Errors aren't personal.
Python never gets personal with you.
They just feel personal.

SyntaxError: The Classic Slap on the Wrist

The first error every beginner meets is SyntaxError, the friendly neighborhood reminder that Python is particular about how you speak to it.

You forget a parenthesis?
SyntaxError.

You mistype a keyword?
SyntaxError.

You breathe wrong near your colon?
SyntaxError.

This is Python's way of saying, "I see what you tried to do, and I admire the effort, but the answer is still no."

Favorite subgenre:

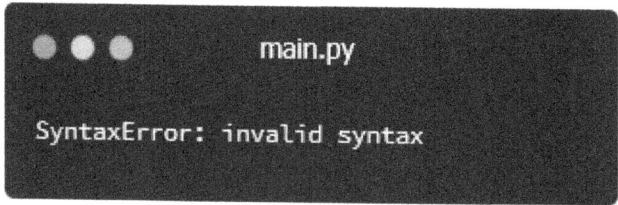

Thank you, Python.
I, too, enjoy vague criticism.

NameError: Python Has No Idea What You're Talking About

This one happens when you try to use a variable that doesn't exist.

Translation:

"You spelled it wrong. Again."

Python doesn't judge your spelling... but it kind of does.

NameError is responsible for 83% of all developer self-doubt. (The other 17% is pip-related.)

TypeError: You Mixed the Wrong Ingredients

TypeError appears when you treat values in ways that make Python question your reasoning abilities.

```
● ● ●                    main.py

TypeError: can only concatenate str (not "int") to str
```

This is Python's gentle suggestion that you should reconsider your life choices.

Beginners often ask:

"Why doesn't Python just convert it for me?"

Because Python wants you to learn, not succeed too quickly. Python might be easy, but not that easy.

ImportError: When Python Refuses to Acknowledge Your Work

ImportError happens for many reasons:

- the file doesn't exist
- the file exists but isn't in the right folder
- the file is in the right folder, but Python is in a mood

ImportError teaches an essential lesson:

Just because you know where your files are doesn't mean Python does.

This is the error that makes you question the very concept of "directories."

The Iconic IndentationError

This is the one.
The myth.
The legend.
The master of bugs.

IndentationError is Python's signature move, the one problem that every single developer encounters regardless of experience.

One rogue space...
one sneaky tab...
one indentation level off by a hair...

And suddenly Python reacts like you insulted its ancestors:

```
● ● ●                main.py

IndentationError: unexpected indent
```

This is the moment beginners discover that Python cares deeply about whitespace.
Too deeply.

Veteran developers experience indentation errors the same way seasoned soldiers react to fireworks: sudden tension, flashbacks, questionable breathing patterns.

IndentationError is not an error.
It's a rite of passage.

"It Works on My Machine": The Veteran's Battle Cry

At some point, you will write code that runs perfectly on your computer and breaks violently everywhere else.

This is not technically an error message, but it might as well be tattooed onto the forehead of every developer who's ever collaborated with another human being.

Your code works locally? Great.
Deploy it and watch it scream.

This is where you learn about:

- different Python versions

- different environments

- dependencies you didn't know you had

- dependencies you didn't know you lost

- that one hidden config file you forgot existed

When you say, "It works on my machine," what you really mean is, "I refuse to accept responsibility for this situation."

Errors Don't Make You a Bad Developer

This is the part most people never say out loud:

Everyone gets errors.
Everyone gets stuck.
Everyone stares at their screen whispering, "But... why?"

Beginners, entry-level Pythonistas, well-seasoned ones, and the so-called Python experts, all do meet errors daily.

Errors are not the enemy.
Errors are the conversation between you and the interpreter.

They guide you.
They frustrate you.
They shape you.
They slowly erode your sanity.

But they also make you better.

When you see an error, especially a big dramatic one, remember:

You're not alone.
Every Pythonista has been here.
Every Pythonista will be here again.

Errors are simply proof that you're coding.

And coding, my friend, is messy business.

PART 2
EARLY PAIN: LEARNING JUST
ENOUGH TO BREAK EVERYTHING

CHAPTER 5

Debugging: The Emotional Stages for All Levels

Debugging is not a technical activity.
Debugging is an emotional journey with occasional logic sprinkled in if you're lucky.

When your code breaks, you don't just fix it.
You cycle through denial, anger, bargaining, depression, and acceptance at least twice before lunch.

Every developer, beginner to veteran, experiences the same five stages.
The only difference is how quickly you scream.

Let's walk through it together.

Stage 1: Denial: "This should work."

You run your code.
It breaks.

You stare at the error message as if staring will intimidate it into disappearing.

"This doesn't make sense," you whisper.
"I literally didn't change anything."

Spoiler:
You did change something.
You changed something very stupid, but we'll get to that later.

Denial is that hopeful moment when you believe the problem is temporary.
A glitch in the Matrix.

Sunspots.
Cosmic rays.
Anything but your code.

Stage 2: Anger: "Why are you like this?!"

Denial doesn't last long.

Soon you slam headfirst into anger.

You start blaming:

- Python
- your editor
- the computer
- your past self
- your future self
- whoever invented whitespace
- even Guido van Rossum

If you're a beginner, you blame yourself.
If you're a veteran, you blame the universe.

Both are reasonable responses.

At this point you might say things like:

"I've done everything right."
"This should NOT be happening."
"WHY is it always the colon?"

And Python sits quietly, unfazed, because it has seen millions like you and will see millions more.

Stage 3: Bargaining: "If this works, I'll be a better person."

This is when you start trying random things:

- adding parentheses
- removing parentheses
- deleting lines
- restoring lines
- spacing things out
- un-spacing things
- renaming variables for no reason
- trying print() in 42 places thinking "maybe 42 really is the answer to everything"

You even start negotiating with the machine.

"If this works now, I will...
clean up my code...
stop Googling everything...
never curse at Python again...
I'll never forget to tick the Windows PATH checkbox again...
maybe."

You don't mean any of it.
Python knows it.
And maybe it's the reason why it doesn't care about your bargaining.

Stage 4: Depression: "I'm not built for this."

This is the darkest stage.

You slump in your chair.

You stare out the window like a Victorian poet contemplating the fragility of life.

"I'm not smart enough for this."
"Maybe carpentry wasn't such a bad idea."
"People who code for fun must be emotionally unwell."

You Google error messages and find ancient forum posts from 2009 where someone had your exact problem but never replied with the solution.

You feel personally betrayed.

This stage lasts anywhere from five minutes to twenty years.

Stage 5: Acceptance: "Fine. Let's just fix it."

Eventually, something shifts.

You wipe the emotional sweat from your forehead and decide to read the error message more carefully.

And there it is:

The answer.

The missing colon.
The wrong variable name.
The function you forgot to call.
The tab that snuck in like a ninja.
The single letter that ruined your morning.

You fix it.
Your code runs.

You are reborn.

For exactly three minutes, until the next bug appears and the cycle begins again.

Debugging Styles: Choose Your Fighter

Every developer eventually develops a signature debugging method. None of them are healthy.

The Print() Surgeon

Adds print statements everywhere like band-aids on bad decisions.

The Code Deleter

Deletes giant sections of code until the bug stops happening and then quietly pretends it was intentional.

The Staring Monk

Does not touch the keyboard.
Does not move.
Just stares at the code until the bug confesses out of fear.

The Rewrite Evangelist

Solves all bugs by rewriting everything from scratch, even if the issue was a single misplaced parenthesis.

The StackOverflow Pilgrim

Searches for enlightenment in ancient posts, following the sacred wisdom of strangers who may or may not have been sober.

You Are Normal

Every developer debugged like this.
Every developer still debug like this.
Even experts get stuck on ridiculous bugs that make them question their career.

Debugging feels messy because it is messy.
It's not a failure.
It's the core activity of programming.

If you debug, you are a real programmer.
If you suffer while doing it, you're a real Python programmer.

And that's a badge of honor.

CHAPTER 6
Loops: Beginners Repeat Too Much, Pros Repeat Too Much But Elegantly

Loops are where Python programmers first encounter real power.
Not gentle power like print().
More like "I just told the computer to repeat something a hundred times and now the fan is screaming."

Beginners love loops.
Pros fear them in a quiet, experienced way.

Both groups are correct.

The Beginner's First Loop
The first time a beginner writes:

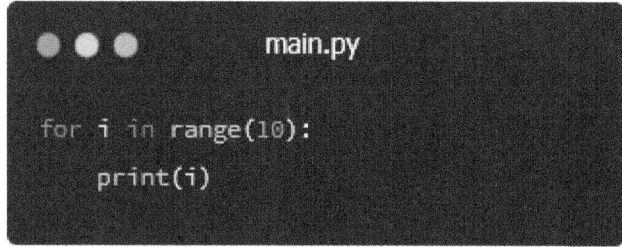

```
for i in range(10):
    print(i)
```

they sit back and whisper, "I have mastered the machine!" with arms raised as if they've won the Code Challenge Championship.

This is the honeymoon period.
Beginners feel unstoppable.
They start looping all kinds of things because now everything needs to be repeated.

Names? Loop them.
Emails? Loop them.
Lists that should never be looped? Loop them anyway.

Beginners don't fear infinite loops.

Beginners don't know about infinite loops.

They are truly blessed.

The Off-by-One Curse

Loops introduce the first mathematical trauma of Python programming: the off-by-one error.

You write a loop expecting it to run 10 times.
It runs 9.
Or 11.
Or it breaks the fabric of reality.

Somewhere between range(10) and your expectations lies a tiny pit of confusion where countless developers have fallen.

Every Pythonista eventually screams:

"WHY DOESN'T THIS END AT 10?!"

Python, calmly:

"I did exactly what you said."

Infinite Loops: The Soundtrack of Panic

Then comes the moment every beginner meets their first infinite loop.
You didn't mean to make an infinite loop.
It just... happened to you.

You run the code.
The output floods your screen like a waterfall of regret.

Your CPU starts warming up.
Your laptop fans kick in like you just launched a space shuttle.

You panic.
You slam Ctrl+C repeatedly like you're trying to break out of handcuffs.

Every developer remembers the first time they felt true fear, and it usually involved a loop gone rogue.

Veterans Don't Avoid Mistakes. They Make Prettier Ones.

Pros write compact, elegant loops, the kind that beginners stare at like ancient runes.

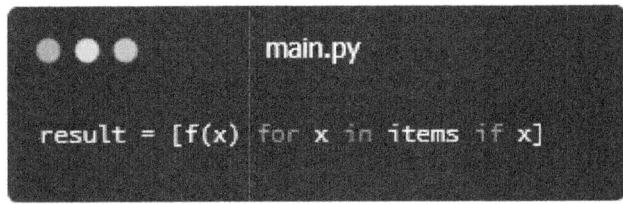

```python
result = [f(x) for x in items if x]
```

Beginners scream:

"What does this even mean?!"

Veterans shrug:

"It's a list comprehension."

Nobody fully understands list comprehensions.
We just accept them as Python's attempt at modern art.

They're shorter.
They're cleaner.
They hide mistakes more effectively.

A win is a win.

Nested Loops: The Silent CPU Killer

There comes a time when a developer tries nesting loops:

```
● ● ●              main.py

for i in items:
    for j in items2:
        do_something(i, j)
```

You think you're writing simple code.
But you've actually created a device capable of bringing mid-range laptops to their knees.

Nested loops scale fast.

Too fast.

Wildly fast.

One day you will run nested loops so carelessly that your computer will freeze and you'll sit there waiting, wondering whether:

- the code is running
- the code has crashed
- or you have transcended linear time

The answers are usually: yes, yes, and yes.

While Loops: The Developer Trust Fall

The while loop is Python's way of asking:

"Do you trust yourself?"

Because Python is giving you full control over when the loop ends.
This is dangerous.
Developers are not known for responsible decision-making.

One forgotten update inside the loop and you've got yourself an infinite existential crisis.

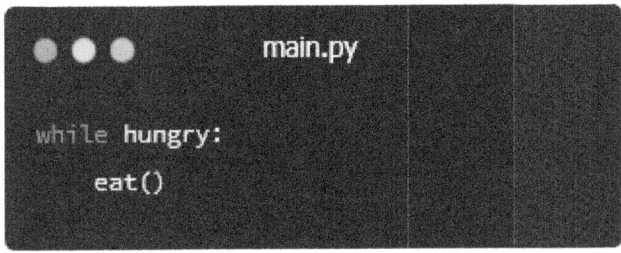

Theoretically this ends.
In reality... maybe not.

The Evolution of a Pythonista Through Loops

Here's the lifecycle:

Beginner

Writes loops too long.
Loops everything.
Breaks machines.

Intermediate

Discovers list comprehensions.
Feels clever.
Feels powerful.
Forgets to handle edge cases.

Veteran

Writes one-line loops so compact that even they don't understand them six months later.

Then blames past-them for writing such unreadable nonsense.

Both of them are correct.

You Don't Have To Be Perfect

Loops are not a test of intelligence.
They're a test of patience.

You will:

- write messy loops
- crash programs
- freeze laptops
- misunderstand range()
- create infinite loops unintentionally
- create infinite loops intentionally, because sometimes you need that in some periods of life

It's normal.
It's part of the journey.

Loops are like training wheels for actual complexity, preparing you for a future filled with recursion, generators, and async functions that require emotional counseling.

For now, just know this:

If you've broken a loop, you're a real Python programmer.

And if you've broken two, welcome to the Fine Pythonistas club.

CHAPTER 7
Functions: Organization for People Who Don't Feel Like Organizing

Functions are supposed to make your code cleaner. That's the sales pitch.

"Put code into reusable blocks," they say. "It'll make everything tidy," they say.

And then you meet your first real function and realize you've essentially created a tiny, moody creature that refuses to behave unless you give it exactly what it wants in exactly the right format.

Welcome to functions, where control is an illusion and arguments are not just parameters, they're what you will be having with your code for the next several years.

Beginners Don't Use Functions

In the beginning, beginners write everything at the top level of the file. Everything.

Your program starts to look like a grocery list someone dropped down a staircase:

```
● ● ●                    main.py

name = input("Enter name: ")
print("Hello,", name)


age = int(input("Enter age: "))
print("Next year you'll be", age + 1)


# …hundreds of lines later…
```

It's a beautiful mess.

No structure.
No organization.
Just pure, chaotic storytelling.

And honestly?
There is innocence in that kind of freedom.

Intermediates Use Too Many Functions

Something changes once a beginner decides to "get serious."

They've watched a YouTube tutorial.
They've read a blog post.
They think, "Real programmers use functions."

And suddenly every piece of logic, no matter how microscopic, gets shoved into a function.

```
● ● ●                main.py

def ask_user_name():
    return input("What is your name? ")

def print_greeting(name):
    print("Hello,", name)

def main():
    name = ask_user_name()
    print_greeting(name)

main()
```

Does this need functions?

No.

Will the intermediate stop?

Also no.

These are the golden months where developers treat functions like decorative pillows: unnecessary but placed everywhere anyway.

Veterans Use Functions Like Russian Nesting Dolls

Veterans embrace functions, but not in a calm, healthy way.

They create functions that call other functions that call other functions which call something named helper_inner_process_core() and now the stack trace is a novel.

You try to follow the logic and end up feeling like you're reading a mystery book where every chapter ends with a cliffhanger.

Veterans don't build programs.
They build labyrinths.

They call it "architecture."

Arguments: The Negotiation Stage

Functions can take arguments.

In theory, this is simple.

In practice, arguments start to feel like a heated discussion where Python demands:

"Tell me EXACTLY what you want me to work with."

For beginners, arguments are mysterious.

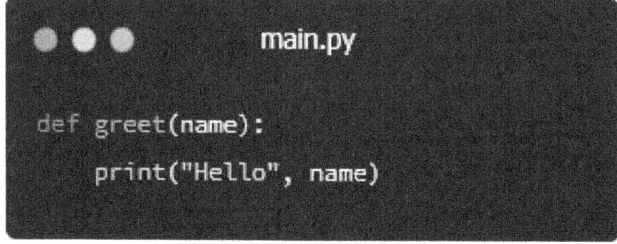

```
● ● ●                main.py

def greet(name):
    print("Hello", name)
```

They look at name inside the parentheses and whisper:

"So... does Python just... know what that is?"

Not yet, my friend. Not yet.

For intermediates, arguments are where confusion multiplies:

- positional arguments
- keyword arguments
- *args
- **kwargs

*args and **kwargs deserve their own chapter, because they're basically Python saying:

"I'm not explaining this. You'll figure it out eventually. Hopefully."

Return Values: Optional... Until They Aren't

First-time developers forget to return things.

All the time.

```
● ● ●                main.py

def add(a, b):
    print(a + b)
```

This works, sure.
But try to use that result:

```
● ● ●                main.py

result = add(2, 3)
```

Now *result* is *None*.

48

Somewhere far away, a senior developer feels a disturbance in the force.

Veterans, on the other hand, return values from functions like they're running a shipping warehouse:

```
● ● ●              main.py

return value, other_value, some_flag,
metadata, this_thing, that_thing
```

You unpack it and suddenly half your screen is variable assignments.

Functions grow up fast.

Scope: Or "Why Can't You See My Variables?"

Function scope is where beginners first experience betrayal.

You set a variable outside the function.
You try to use it inside the function.
Python says, "Nope."

You set a variable inside the function.
You try to use it outside the function.
Python says, "Nope."

Suddenly you're in a custody battle with your own variables.

This is how programmers learn the word "scope."
Not from a tutorial, but from grief.

The Moment Everything Clicks

Eventually, after dozens of painful attempts and at least one meltdown involving TypeError: missing 1 required positional argument, something happens.

Functions start to make sense.

You realize they're not about organization or neatness.

They're about sanity.

Because once you can break your code into understandable pieces...
you can breathe.

You can think.

You can avoid scrolling through 900 lines of spaghetti just to fix one bug.

Functions won't save your life, but they'll keep you from losing it.

You're Doing Great

No one writes perfect functions at first.
Or later.
Or ever.

You just get better at hiding the chaos inside them.

And that's programming.

If your functions work, even if they're held together by hope and print statements, you're doing better than half the internet.

Take the win.

CHAPTER 8
Imports: How Pythonistas "Borrow" Genius

Imports are Python's version of looking at your code, shrugging, and saying, "Someone else has probably done this better."

They're not just a feature.
They're a lifestyle.
A survival strategy.

In Python, you don't reinvent the wheel.
You import a wheel, attach a few extras, and congratulate yourself on being resourceful.

Beginners Import with Shy Enthusiasm

The first import a beginner ever writes is usually:

They don't know why they're doing it.
They don't know what it means.
They just know the tutorial said to.

Then they write:

```
● ● ●                main.py

print(random.randint(1, 10))
```

And suddenly they're magicians.

Beginners love this moment.
It's the first taste of power that *isn't* tied to loops or print()
therapy.

They think:

"I can import anything!"

Oh, sweet summer child.

Pros Import Half the Universe

Veterans don't import one thing.
Veterans import like they're stocking a bunker for winter.

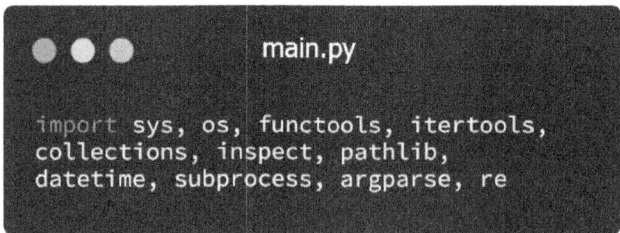

```
● ● ●                main.py

import sys, os, functools, itertools,
collections, inspect, pathlib,
datetime, subprocess, argparse, re
```

They don't even look at the list.
They've been importing these modules since the Bronze Age.

Some of them the developer won't even use.

They just import them preemptively, like seasoning a dish
before you even know what you're cooking.

The Moment Beginners Realize Imports Are Just... Other People's Code

There's always a moment, a quiet, horrifying moment, when a beginner learns that imports are just files.
Other people's files.

They realize "Python" isn't one clean, unified language. It's a collection of functions duct-taped together across the planet.

Some beginner out there always whispers:

"Wait... does that mean someone wrote math.sin()?"

Yes.
A human being wrote that.
Probably while tired.
Possibly while regretting their career choices.

And now you're using it like it's a magical command from the heavens.

Imports are trust falls with strangers.

Packages vs Modules: The Confusion Olympics

Here's where Python starts testing your sanity.

A **module** is a file.
A **package** is a folder.
A **library** is a collection of packages.
And **pip** is the questionable mechanism that installs them and occasionally breaks your entire environment.

Beginners try to understand this and their eyes glaze over like they've been hit with a tranquilizer dart.

Pros don't understand either.
They just bluff confidently.

The Fear of ImportError

ImportError is Python's way of saying:

"I see you're trying to use that thing...
but I don't see that thing."

It feels personal.

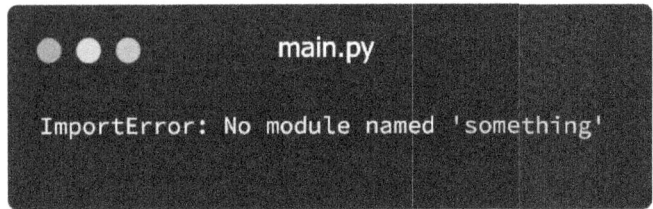

You're sure it exists.
You swear you installed it.
You remember doing it.

You Google solutions.
You reinstall the package.
You reinstall Python.
You consider reinstalling yourself.

Sometimes the fix is simple.
Sometimes the fix is "you installed it in the wrong virtual
environment, you fool."

"from X import Y": A Gateway to Overconfidence

At some point, beginners discover a new toy:

Nothing bad happens.

They get bold.

They start importing everything directly:

And then one day, they do this:

Veterans see it and gasp like someone dropped a baby.

Importing everything is chaos.
It dumps clutter into your namespace.
It breaks autocomplete.
It confuses the reader.
It makes your variables fight each other like jealous siblings.

Veterans treat import * the same way adults treat glitter:
once it's in your project, you'll never get rid of it.

The Magical Realism of init.py

Every Python developer eventually stumbles onto an __init__.py file and whispers:

"What... what are you?"

It looks important.
It behaves mysteriously.
It controls your package imports like a mafia boss.

And nobody really explains it.
You just accept its existence like a cosmic constant and move on.

The Truth: Imports Are Python's Greatest Superpower

Imports let you build apps in hours instead of months.
They let you use the labor of thousands of extremely exhausted developers across the world.

They're messy.
They're confusing.
They're occasionally violent.

But they give Python its magic.

Every time you import something, you are reaching out to the entire global Python community and saying:

"Hey, I'm stealing your work. Thanks."

And that's beautiful.

Chapter 9
Googling Like a Pro (AKA 90% of Coding)

The biggest lie in programming is that you need to know everything.

You don't.

You need to **Google** everything.

Google is the true programming language.
Python is just the syntax you use once you've found the correct StackOverflow answer from 2013.

Beginners Google Cute Things

Beginners type things like:

- "how to sort a list python"
- "python list reverse"
- "why does python say unexpected indent"
- "how do i make a calculator in python easy"

The search engine pats them on the head and gives them exactly what they need.

Google loves beginners.
Beginners ask straightforward questions.
Beginners are wholesome.

Veterans?
Veterans are a different story.

Pros Google War Crimes

As a developer gains experience, their search history turns into a psychological thriller.

- "python list sort weird behavior why"
- "python remove ghost environments help"
- "pip broke my python again fix pls"
- "asyncio event loop died? who killed it"
- "python program works then stops working reasons???"
- "NONE TYPE ERROR WHY"
- "regex not working even though it should be working it should WHY ISN'T IT WORKING"

These aren't searches.
These are emotional outbursts.

Google knows this.
Google sighs and puts on its rubber gloves.

Everyone Googles the Same Five Things

It doesn't matter if you're a complete beginner or a senior architect with three coffee machines and a standing desk. You will Google these exact topics forever:

1. **How to sort a list**
   You will forget.
   And half the time you're not even sorting the right list anyway... because you named it something unhelpful like data_final_FINAL_really_final3 back in Chapter 3. Past-you strikes again.
   You find the answer and say, "Ah, that's how it's done!"
   You will forget again.
   This is the circle of life.

2. **How to exit a virtual environment**
   Nobody remembers.
   Not even Python.

3. **Regex**
   Every developer searches "regex cheat sheet" at least twice a week.

4. **How to install a package properly**
   Trick question:
   You can't.

5. **StackOverflow**
   Not a topic, but a coping mechanism.

StackOverflow: The Programmer's Shrine

Every Pythonista eventually ends up on StackOverflow, reading an answer from a mythical creature named "user2817742" who solved the problem in three lines of cryptic brilliance.

You copy the solution.
You paste it into your code.
You don't understand it.
It works anyway.

You whisper:

"Thank you, mysterious stranger."

This is normal.
This is healthy.
This is modern software engineering.

The Dark Art of Reading Error Messages

At some point, beginners discover that you can copy-paste error messages directly into Google and get solutions instantly.

Veterans know this.
Veterans copy entire traceback logs like they're dumping confessions into an AI therapist.

"python ValueError: too many values to unpack expected 2 got 3 fix???"

Google doesn't judge.
Google has seen worse.
Google *is* worse.

Why Googling Is Not Cheating

Let's be clear:

Googling is not cheating. It's the job.

Programming is not about memorizing everything.
It's about knowing that someone, somewhere, already solved the weird problem you're having and generously posted it online without realizing that ten years later you would be clinging to their answer like a life raft.

Real Python (and general programming) skills:

- knowing what to search

- knowing how to skim answers

- knowing when the person answering is wrong but confident

- knowing when you yourself are wrong but confident

- and learning to live with both

Googling is not a sign of weakness.
It's a sign you're a real developer.

The Search Spiral

Every programmer eventually goes through the Search Spiral:

1. Search for solution
2. Read StackOverflow
3. Try solution
4. Break something else
5. Search again
6. Open documentation
7. Consider giving up
8. Watch a tutorial
9. Open 14 tabs
10. Forget the original question
11. Restart computer
12. Suddenly realize the fix was a missing parenthesis

The Spiral is eternal.
We all walk the path.
We all survive.

PART 3
THE VETERAN YEARS: WELCOME TO THE DARK SIDE

CHAPTER 10

When You Meet Classes and Understand Nothing for 6 to 12 Months

Classes are the point in your Python journey where the language smiles politely, hands you a stack of new concepts, and whispers:

"Good luck, champion."

Everybody struggles with classes.
Everybody.
It does not matter how smart you are, how many tutorials you watch, or how many times you say, "Okay, I think I get it now."

You don't.
Not yet.
And that's normal.

Beginners Look at Classes Like Ancient Texts

At first, you see something like this:

```
● ● ●                    main.py

class Dog:
    def __init__(self, name):
        self.name = name

    def bark(self):
        print(self.name, "says woof!")
```

And your first thought is:

"What... is this structure? Why is everything indented like a staircase? And why is this self person everywhere?"

You scroll through documentation, and every explanation starts sounding like a riddle from a fantasy novel:

- "A class is a blueprint."

- "Objects are instances of classes."

- "self refers to the current instance."

Beginners nod politely while internally screaming:

"I'm sorry, what?!"

Classes are your first real taste of object-oriented programming.
And object-oriented programming is the moment you begin lying.
Not to others, but to yourself.

"I understand this," you say confidently.
You do not.

The Great Identity Crisis Called self

Let's talk about the elephant in the room.

self

Every class has it.
Every method takes it.
Nobody explains why without making the explanation even more confusing.

Beginners always ask:

"Why do I have to type self every time? Can't Python already tell it's inside the class?"

The answer is yes.
Python can tell.
Python just chooses not to.

self is Python's way of saying:

"I know what object you mean, but I want you to say it out loud anyway."

It's like talking to someone who pretends not to hear you unless you use their full name.

Intermediates Pretend They Understand OOP

Once you can write a class without crying, you start feeling confident.

Too confident.

You start throwing classes everywhere:

```
● ● ●              main.py

class Calculator:
    def add(self, a, b):
        return a + b
```

Does this need a class?
Absolutely not.

Will you use a class anyway?
Absolutely yes.

This phase lasts months.
Sometimes years.
You are building object-oriented monuments to concepts that should have been simple functions.

Veterans Use Classes Like Loaded Weapons

Seasoned developers treat classes with both respect and suspicion.

They know classes can be powerful.
They also know classes can pull the pin on their sanity if misused.

Veterans build:

- inheritance hierarchies
- chains of subclasses
- mixins
- factories
- abstract base classes

At some point you'll see something like:

```
class Duck(Flyable, Quackable,
JSONSerializable):
```

And you'll whisper:

"No. No, no, no. What have you done?"

Veterans look back at you with quiet, haunted eyes and say:

"It made sense at the time."

Inheritance: The Staircase to Confusion

Inheritance seems simple:

"You create a class inside another class."

No.
Incorrect.
Stop.

Inheritance is where your architecture becomes a Russian nesting doll of questionable decisions.

You try to follow the flow:

A inherits B, B inherits C, C overrides something from D, D calls something from A...

Your brain reboots.

You close the file.
You go for a walk.
You reconsider your career and life choices.

The Moment When Classes Finally Make Sense

Here's the truth nobody tells beginners:

Classes don't "click" the first time.
Not the tenth time.
Not even the fiftieth time.

At some point, usually while building a project, you suddenly realize:

"Oh. Oh! Classes are just... ways to group data and behavior together."

The fog lifts.
The explanation actually lands.
Everything that felt cryptic starts looking... reasonable.

This moment is the programming equivalent of enlightenment.

You have scaled the mountain.
You have seen the view.

You still don't fully understand inheritance, but nobody does, so it's fine.

You're Not Supposed to Get It Immediately

Classes are the first real obstacle where beginners wonder:

"Am I cut out for this?"

Yes.
You are.

You're not confused because you're bad at coding.
You're confused because classes are confusing.

Everyone who has ever learned Python has stared at a class for hours wondering why it exists and what it even does.

Then one day it clicks.
And when it clicks, it stays.

So, breathe.
Be patient.
And never forget:

Even the pros Google "Python class examples for beginners" every now and then.

CHAPTER 11

The Package Ecosystem: Heaven, Hell, and pip install BrokenMyPython

Python's package ecosystem is both the best thing about Python...
and the reason some developers wake up at 3 AM in a cold sweat.

It's a magical land of reusable code.
It's also a haunted forest full of dependency monsters, cursed virtual environments, and packages that stopped updating somewhere around 2017.

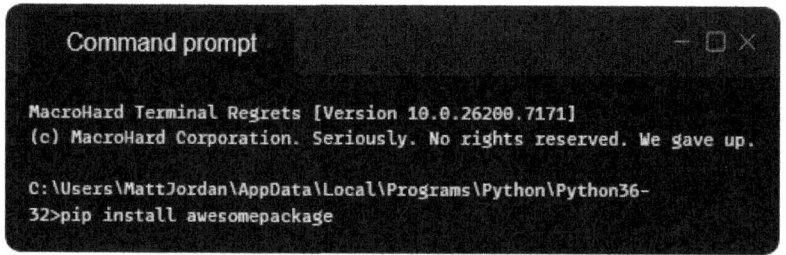

It installs.
It works.
You feel powerful.

Beginners walk around confidently installing things like:

- numpy
- requests
- pandas

They have no idea they're summoning ancient beasts that want very specific versions of everything.

Beginners believe pip is reliable.

Veterans know pip is a gamble with emotional consequences.

The Moment It All Starts Falling Apart

One day you type:

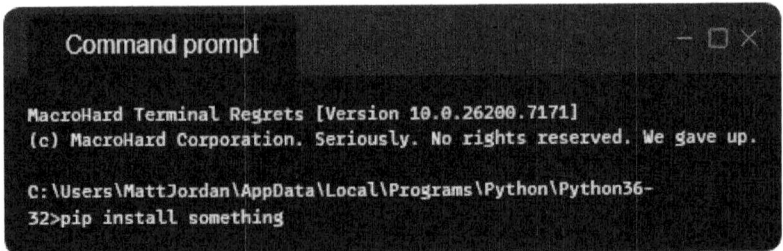

And pip says:

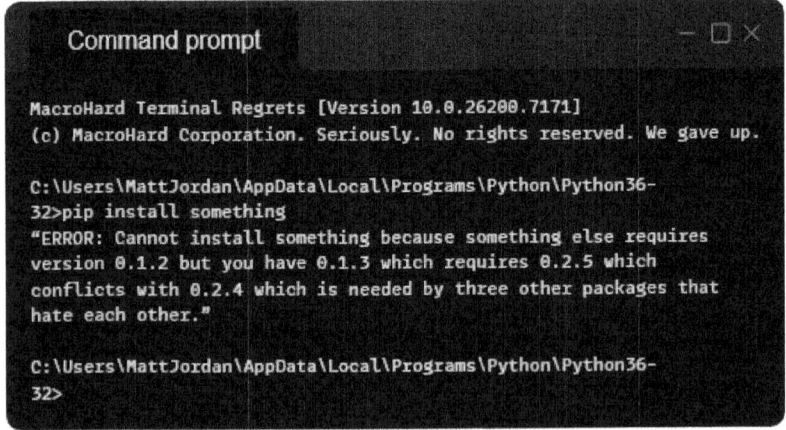

You stare at your screen.

You wonder if you should cry or just accept death peacefully.

This, dear reader, is dependency hell.

The Rise of the Virtual Environment

Every Python tutorial eventually introduces the idea of virtual environments, which are described as:

"Isolated folders that keep your packages separate."

But what they really are is:

"Tiny ecosystems with their own needs, moods, and ability to corrupt themselves without warning."

Beginners try this:

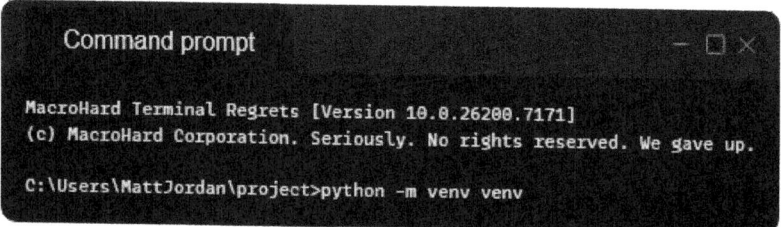

Then activate it:

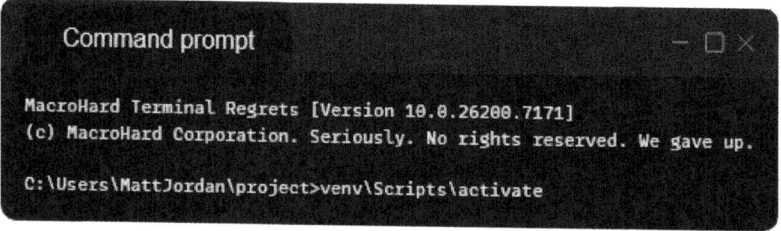

(or if you're on Mac/Linux and like suffering:)

"*source venv/bin/activate*"

Beginners feel proud.

Veterans know this environment is a ticking bomb.

The Ghost Environment Phenomenon

Eventually you install a package...
and it doesn't appear.
Or it appears somewhere else.
Or Python pretends it never happened.

You end up with 6 environments:

- the one you created
- the one you meant to create
- the one VS Code made secretly
- the one PyCharm created without asking
- the global one you swore you weren't using
- the mysterious one you have no memory of ever making

You run pip list and see a package you didn't install.

You ask, "Where did this come from?"

No answer.

Just silence.

Python environments are not tools.
They are cryptids.

Version Conflicts: The Dance of Doom

At some point you install a package that requires an older version of another package that requires a newer version of a third package, and now you're in a dependency sandwich nobody ordered.

You try to fix it manually:

```
Command prompt                                      −  □  ×

MacroHard Terminal Regrets [Version 10.0.26200.7171]
(c) MacroHard Corporation. Seriously. No rights reserved. We gave up.

C:\Users\MattJordan\AppData\Local\Programs\Python\Python36-
32>pip install "something==1.4.2"
```

But now the other package breaks.

You fix that package.

The first one breaks again.

This is Python's version of whack-a-mole.
A very sad version.

The Veteran's Strategy

Pros do not fear pip.
They respect it like a dangerous animal.

Veteran workflow:

1. Create virtual environment
2. Install exactly the packages needed
3. Freeze them
4. Never touch anything again
5. Pray

You'll see experienced developers refuse to upgrade a package for five years because:

"It works right now and I'm afraid to disturb it."

This is wisdom.

pip install is a Gamble

Every pip command is an emotional bet:

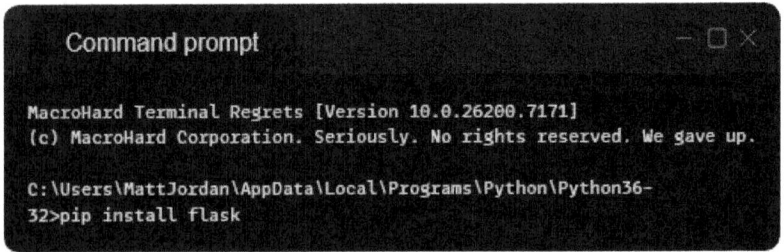

Outcome possibilities:

- it works
- it installs the wrong version
- it installs globally by accident
- it breaks something important
- it overwrites something vital
- it summons a conflict from 2018

pip is not a package manager.

pip is a casino.

"It Works on Python 3.8.2": The Prophecy

Some projects require very specific versions of Python:

- 3.8.2
- 3.9.13
- 3.10.7-but-not-3.10.8-for-some-reason

You install a newer version thinking "What could go wrong?"

Everything.

Everything could go wrong.

Python versioning is the part of programming where even senior engineers start mumbling to themselves.

But Here's the Beautiful Truth

Despite the chaos, the Python package ecosystem is one of the most powerful in the world.

Want to do machine learning?
Install it.

Want to scrape the web?
Install it.

Want to build a website?
Install it.

Want to cause emotional harm to yourself with async?
Install it.

Python's ecosystem is messy, chaotic, and occasionally hostile, but it's also overflowing with brilliance created by thousands of developers who suffered so you wouldn't have to.

Well...
you still have to.
But at least they suffered first.

CHAPTER 12
Async: The Chapter Where Even Seniors Cry

Async is Python's way of saying:

"Feeling confident? Let's fix that."

Then it pulls out a second timeline, a parallel universe, three event loops, and a function that doesn't run when you call it, and whispers:

"Not anymore."

Async is powerful.
Async is elegant.
Async is the reason otherwise stable developers lie awake at 2 AM reconsidering their career path.

Beginners' First Reaction: "Why isn't this running?"

Your first async function looks so innocent:

```
● ● ●              main.py

async def hello():
    print("Hello")


hello()
```

You expect it to work.
It does not.

Instead, Python gives you that classic vibe:

"Oh, sweet child... you thought that would actually run? How adorable."

Async functions don't run unless you await them:

But you can't use await unless you're inside another async function.

So now you need:

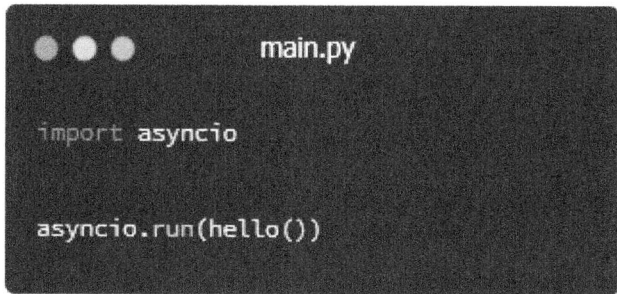

And this is the moment beginners realize async isn't a feature. It's an initiation ritual.

The Veteran Reaction: Full-Body Shudder

Experienced developers see async code and physically tense up.

It's the same look they give merge conflicts or IKEA assembly instructions that say "attach screw C into slot Q using tool X that does not exist in the physical realm."

They know async can make things fast.
They also know async can make things very, very broken.

Async issues don't fail loudly.
They fail... silently.
Like a ninja removing a floorboard while you're standing on it.

The Event Loop: Python's Secret Rollercoaster

Async introduces something called **the event loop**.

This is where Python runs tasks in a swirling, magical tornado of non-blocking execution that absolutely nobody fully understands.

You ask:

"What is the event loop?"

The real answer:

"A mysterious circle of execution that must not be disturbed."

The developers who built it?
Brilliant.
The rest of us?
We just pray it doesn't get upset.

await: The Word You Use Incorrectly for Months

You learn await, and suddenly every piece of code becomes a philosophical question:

Can I await here?

Should I await here?

Why can't I await here?

Why does awaiting here break everything?

Why does not awaiting also break everything?

Why does the error message sound passive-aggressive?

Using await correctly feels like solving a riddle written by a poet who hates clarity.

async def: A Function That Doesn't Behave Like a Function

Beginner expectation:

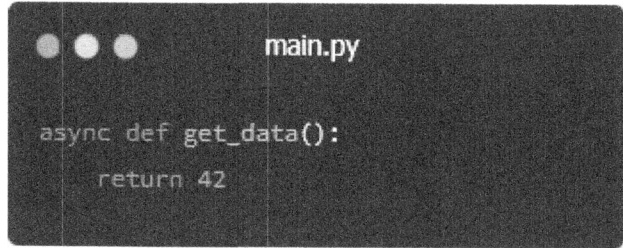

```
async def get_data():
    return 42
```

That should return 42.
Simple, right?

Reality:

It returns a **coroutine object**, also known as:

"A thing you must await or it will haunt your dreams."

Calling an async function is not calling a function.
It's summoning potential.

You haven't done the thing.
You've prepared the idea of doing the thing.

Some people call this "elegant."
Others call it "emotional damage."

The Famous Error: "RuntimeError: Event loop is closed"

At some point you will get this error.

You will not understand it.

Nobody understands it.

Not fully.

This error is Python gently saying:

"You messed with the loop. I told you not to mess with the loop."

Real-World Example of Losing Sanity

You run async code inside Jupyter Notebook.

It works.

You run the exact same code in a script.

It explodes.

You Google it.
The explanations are so long they require a table of contents.

Everyone agrees it's complicated.
Nobody agrees on why.

Debugging Async

Debugging async is like chasing ghosts.
Your code runs out of order.

Errors show up late.
Sometimes never.

You add print statements and feel your soul leave your body as they execute in a sequence that defies Newtonian physics.

You start questioning time itself.

"Did that run before the other thing?"
"Why did that print twice?"
"Am I in a parallel universe?"
"Yes. Probably."

The Ugly Truth

Async is not here to make your life easier.
Async is here to make your program faster while making you slower.

But once you finally understand it...
once you tame the event loop...
once you learn when to await and when not to await...

you unlock a new level of Python power.

Async is the gym membership of programming:
It hurts, you complain constantly, you think about quitting daily... and then one day you look back and realize:

"Oh. I actually get this now."

And Here's the Hopeful Part

If async feels impossible, that's because it is impossible... at first.
Everyone struggles.
Everyone.
EVERYONE.

Even pros mutter things like:

"I swear I knew this last month."

So if you're confused?

You're normal.

If you're overwhelmed?

Welcome to the club.

If you're crying?

You're ahead of schedule.

You'll get there.

And when you do, async becomes one of the most satisfying tools in your Python toolbox.

Just maybe don't start with it.

CHAPTER 13
Decorators: Wizardry You Pretend to Understand

Decorators are Python's version of a magic spell.

Not the cute kind of magic. not card tricks or pulling a rabbit from a hat.

No, decorators are the kind of magic found in dusty books sealed with skull-shaped locks. The kind of magic that grants incredible power but also makes villagers whisper behind your back.

Every Python developer, at some point, encounters decorators and has the same reaction:

"...Nope."

Beginners' First Encounter: "Why Is There an @ Symbol in My Code?"

It always starts innocently.

You're reading some code and suddenly you see this:

```
●  ●  ●           main.py

@some_decorator

def do_something():

    pass
```

And your brain freezes.

"Is this an email address?
Is Python tagging someone?
Is this a comment?
Did I just open a forbidden chapter of the language?"

Decorators are the moment beginners realize Python is hiding deeper levels of nonsense.
They're like learning your cozy little neighborhood has a basement-level nightclub where all the homeowners secretly go after midnight.

The Official Explanation (Which Explains Nothing)

Decorators are usually defined as:

"A callable that takes a function and returns a function."

Right.
Cool.

Thank you for saying words without meaning.

It's like saying a car is "a wheeled transport container for human kinetic relocation."

Technically true.
Emotionally useless.

Beginner translation:

"You put this @-thing above your function, and it suddenly behaves differently. Don't question it."

What Decorators Feel Like

Decorators feel like you're wrapping your function in a very fancy gift box, except the box sometimes changes the gift, sometimes sets it on fire, and other times makes it better in ways you don't fully comprehend.

It's chaos, but the stylish kind.

The Classic Example: Logging

Here's the simple decorator everyone uses as the "easy example":

```python
def logger(func):
    def wrapper(*args, **kwargs):
        print("Calling function:", func.__name__)
        return func(*args, **kwargs)
    return wrapper


@logger
def greet():
    print("Hello!")


greet()
```

You look at this and think:

"So the function is... inside another function... which returns another function... and then we decorate the original function with the wrapper... and then..."

And then your soul quietly steps out for fresh air.

The Moment You Pretend You Understand

At some point, every developer goes through *The Decorator Phase™*, where they confidently say:

"Oh yeah, decorators? Totally get those."

They do not.

Nobody does.

People understand decorators only in the same way people understand mortgages:
enough to use them, not enough to explain them without panicking.

The "Copy-Paste Wizard" Approach

Most developers use decorators like this:

1. Find decorator online
2. Copy decorator
3. Paste decorator
4. Whisper "please work"
5. It works
6. Immediately stop thinking about it forever

This is the healthiest relationship to decorators.

Built-In Decorators: Python's Convenience or Curse

Python has its own built-in decorators, which you'll see and pretend to understand at meetings:

- @staticmethod
- @classmethod
- @property

Half the time you use them correctly.
The other half?
You use them like seasoning.

@property

This one lets you call a method like an attribute.

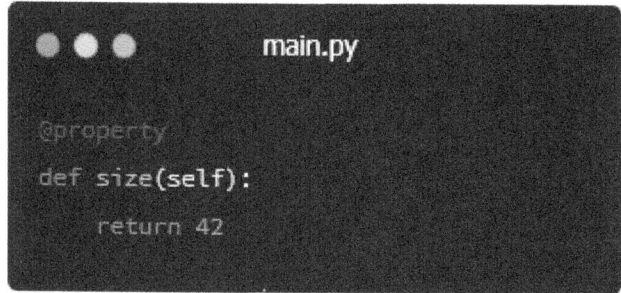

Magical.
Confusing.
Deeply suspicious.

@staticmethod

This decorator says, "I'm in the class but not of the class."

It's the goth teenager of decorators.

@classmethod

This one gives you access to the class instead of the instance.

Beginners: "Why would I need that?"
Pros: "To make architecture worse, obviously."

Advanced Decorators: The Forbidden Arts

Eventually you'll see decorators with arguments:

```python
@retry(times=3)
def connect():
    pass
```

At this point, you are no longer writing Python.

You are practicing ritual magic.

Decorators with arguments require *another* wrapper function around the wrapper function around the original function.

You're basically building a Russian nesting doll of blame.

Debugging Decorators: The Real Horror

Try putting a print statement inside a decorated function.
Watch it run at a moment you did not expect.
Watch your logs turn into a Jackson Pollock painting of confusion and chaos.

Decorators are beautiful.
Decorators are powerful.

Decorators break your brain in ways that force you to rethink your life choices.

But Here's the Beautiful Truth

Once decorators click for you, once you understand that they're just functions modifying functions, you unlock a level of power that makes you feel like the Sorting Hat assigned you to the "Python Wizard" house.

You can:

- inject behavior
- enforce rules
- wrap functionality
- create reusable logic
- manipulate time and space (in code form)

Decorators are advanced tools.
They demand respect.
They demand patience.
They demand at least one cup of coffee per attempt.

But when they work...
oh, they work beautifully.

You Don't Have to Master Them Today if You Are a Beginner

Decorators are not a beginner concept.
They're barely an intermediate concept.

You're allowed to:

- not get them
- half get them
- copy them

- fear them
- avoid them until the stars align

Some developers never fully grasp decorators and still have excellent careers.

They're not a rite of passage.

They're a rite of pain, sure.
But not required pain.

Take your time.
The magic will make sense when you're ready.

CHAPTER 14
Version Control: Git, the Frenemy

Git is not a tool.
Git is a relationship.
A complicated one.
The kind where you love each other, need each other, and occasionally delete each other's progress in a moment of blind panic.

Every Pythonista eventually meets Git, and every Pythonista has the same first impression:

"Oh. Oh no. What... is this?"

Beginners Start With Hope

When beginners first hear about version control, they imagine something simple:

"You save versions of your project. Like checkpoints. So you don't lose work."

They imagine a friendly little button that says:

"Save History ☺ "

Instead, they get commands like:

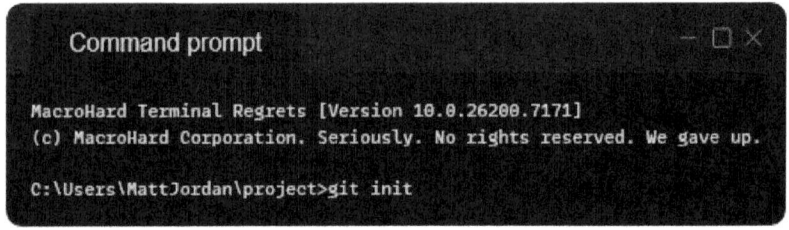

or:

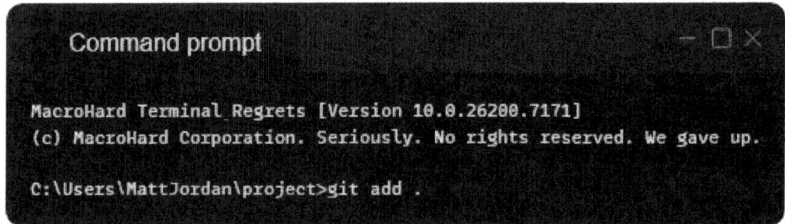

or:

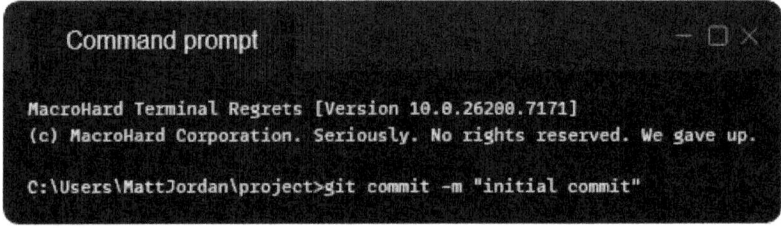

And Git responds with the emotional warmth of a tax auditor.

The First Commit: A Proud, Confusing Moment

Every developer remembers their first commit message.

"initial commit"

It's the default, the classic, the "I have no idea what I'm doing but I want to look professional."

That message will follow you for the rest of your career.
It is your birth certificate in the world of Git.
Treasure it.
Laugh at it.
Fear it.

The Second Commit: Regret Begins

Your second commit message is usually something like:

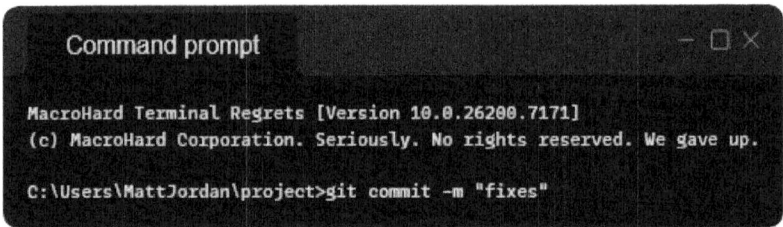

or:

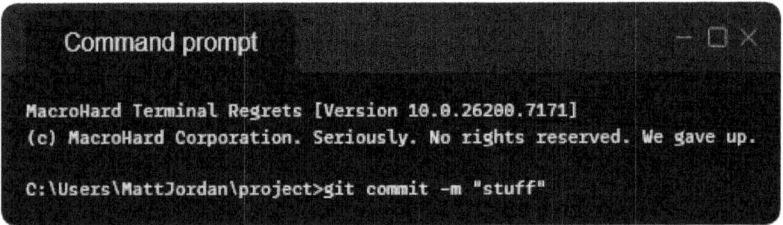

or the truly honest:

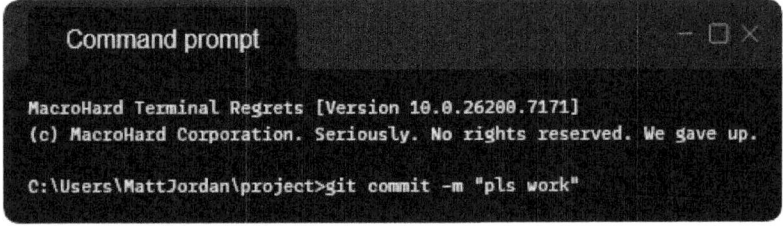

Beginners don't understand what makes a "good commit message."
Veterans do...
but still write bad ones in times of emotional distress.

The First Merge Conflict

A merge conflict is the software equivalent of stepping on a LEGO brick.

You don't know what happened.
You don't know why it hurts.
You only know you want it to stop.

You run:

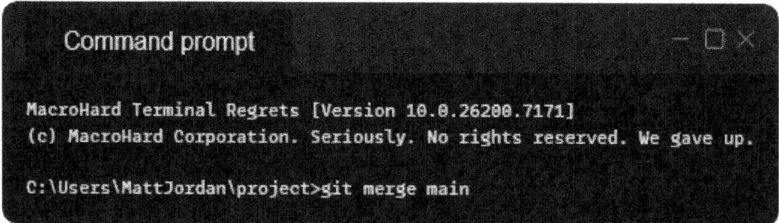

And Git says:

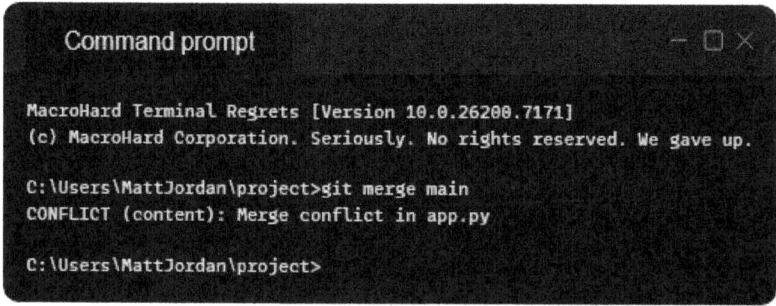

Your soul leaves your body.

A merge conflict is Git telling you:

"You and someone else edited the same thing. Fix it. Fix it yourself. Fix it now!"

Git does not offer comfort.
Git offers responsibility.

The Panic Commands

At some point every developer runs one of these:

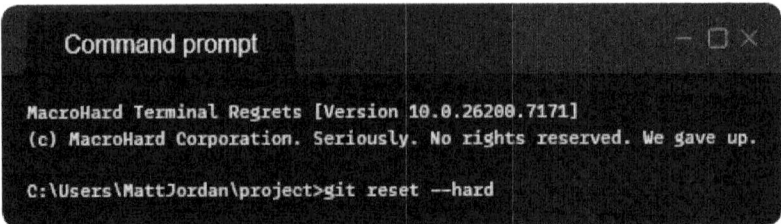

and:

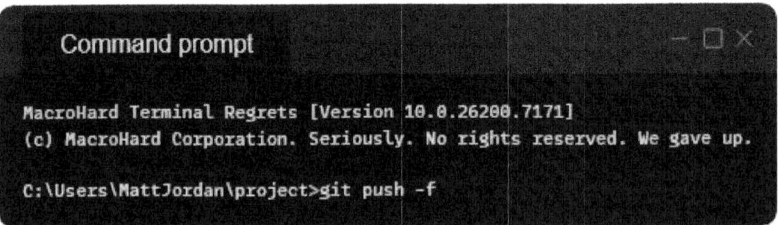

even:

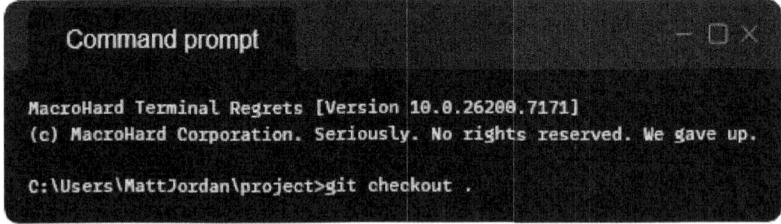

These are not commands.
These are emotional reactions.

Running *git reset --hard* feels like hitting the factory reset button on your life.

Running *git push -f* is like whispering to GitHub:

"I need you to forget everything you thought you knew."

96

Veterans know these commands well.
They use them with caution.
But they still use them.

Branching: A Beautiful Idea That Goes Terribly Wrong

In theory, branching is simple:

"Create a separate line of development."

In practice:

You create a branch.
You create another branch.
Your coworker creates a branch off your branch.
Someone else merges something weird.
You now have:

- main
- dev
- hotfix/auth-bug
- feature/new-ui-final
- feature/new-ui-final-FINAL
- feature/new-ui-final-FINAL-v3
- experimental-do-not-delete-please
- why-do-we-have-so-many-branches

Branching is where Git becomes a family tree drawn by an unmedicated toddler.

Staging: Why Is This Even a Step?

Git makes you "stage" your changes before committing.

Beginners ask:

"Why not just commit?"

Veterans answer:

"Because Git was designed by someone who wanted us to feel things."

Staging is where you discover you've changed 87 files by accident.
None of which you meant to touch.

The Senior Developer Git Style

Veterans use Git with:

- calmness
- precision
- and a wild-west attitude hidden just below the surface

They write commands fast.
They type long messages.
They rebase fearlessly.

But even seniors panic sometimes.
Nothing humbles a developer faster than Git whispering:

"fatal: you are in the middle of a rebase"

Nobody wants to be in the middle of a rebase.
Being in the middle of a rebase is like being in the middle of a thunderstorm wearing metal pajamas.

The Git GUI Phase

Every developer eventually hits the "I'm done with the command line" stage and installs a Git GUI:

- GitKraken
- SourceTree

- GitHub Desktop

Using a GUI feels like stepping out of a war zone and into a spa.

But eventually you return to the command line, because the GUI crashed, and the conflict still needs resolving, and your coworker has pushed something that broke everything again.

Circle of life.

The Truth About Git

Git is powerful.
Git is essential.
Git is unforgiving.

But it's also the thing that saves you when everything breaks.

Git lets you:

- undo mistakes
- track progress
- collaborate
- experiment
- rescue your project at 3 AM
- pretend you know what you're doing

Even though Git drives you insane, it's also the reason your work doesn't disappear forever.

Git is not your friend.
Git is not your enemy.
Git is that strict mentor who constantly yells at you but secretly cares.

And when you finally understand it...
when you fix your first conflict correctly...
when you revert something confidently...

when you troubleshoot a branch that went to war with reality...

you feel powerful.

You become a real engineer.

A slightly traumatized one, sure.
But a real one.

PART 4
PYTHON ENLIGHTENMENT:
THE WISDOM OF THE TIRED

CHAPTER 15
Impostor Syndrome: The Only Constant

Let's get this universally truth fact straight before we go any further:

If you're learning Python and you sometimes feel like you don't belong... you're officially a Python programmer.

Impostor Syndrome isn't a glitch in your journey.
It's a built-in feature of the craft.

Coding feels mysterious.
Python feels easy until it's suddenly not.
Everyone around you seems smarter.
Google autocomplete starts finishing your cries for help before you finish typing them.

This is part of the job.
It's part of the community.
It's the secret handshake we all learn the first time we freeze in front of an error that looks like it's actively judging us.

Beginners Look Around and Assume Everyone Else Knows What They're Doing

Beginners often speak with quiet reverence:

"I just want to reach the point where I understand everything."

I have tragic news for you.

That point does not exist.

You can meet someone with:

- 15 years of experience
- 12 ongoing projects
- 6 open terminals
- and a keyboard that sounds like thunder

...and five minutes later you'll hear them whisper:

"Why... why does this work on Linux but not Windows? Why? Why?!"

Beginners imagine experienced developers floating through problems like sages.

Reality?

We're all Googling the same things you are.
Just with slightly more panic and better coffee.

The First Big Shock: Realizing Python Is Bigger Than You Thought

At first, Python feels small and cozy.

Then one day you stumble across:

- decorators
- generators
- asyncio
- typing
- metaclasses
- something called a "descriptor"
- some cryptic operator you've never seen before

You scroll further and accidentally learn about Numpy, Pandas, Flask, Django, FastAPI, requests, rich, SQLAlchemy, PyTest...

You close your laptop and stare into the void for twenty minutes.

That's the moment impostor syndrome sneaks up behind you and whispers:

"You don't belong here."

Spoiler:
Yes, you do.
That feeling doesn't mean you're failing, it means you've discovered the actual size of the mountain you're climbing.

Welcome to stage two of being a developer:
horrified awareness.

The Intermediate Dilemma: Knowing Enough to Realize You Know Nothing

Intermediates are the most vulnerable to impostor syndrome.

Beginners think:

"I can't do this."

Intermediates think:

"Oh no... I can do this... and that means I can also do it wrong in eighty different ways, and other developers will know."

You suddenly start seeing problems you never noticed before:

"Should I refactor this?"
"Why does my function feel morally wrong?"
"Is this variable name too embarrassing to show anyone?"
"Is async judging me?"

Welcome to the emotional blender.

Intermediates are like teenagers:
they know just enough to get themselves in trouble, but not enough to understand why their parents (senior devs) seem permanently tired.

Seniors Have Impostor Syndrome Too, They've Just Learned to Wear It Like a Jacket

Here's the twist you may not believe yet:

Impostor syndrome gets worse as you improve.

Seniors don't worry about syntax.
They worry about architecture.
They worry about scaling.
They worry about design patterns, team decisions, timelines, and the existential horror of seeing junior developers repeat their old mistakes.

A senior developer will calmly explain a complex system to you...
then go home and Google:

Experience doesn't erase the feeling.
It just turns it into background radiation.

The Comparison Trap: The Silent Killer of Confidence

You scroll the internet and see:

- 17-year-olds building neural networks
- someone writing a full web server in 12 lines
- a person casually solving Advent of Code challenges before breakfast
- that one StackOverflow user who answers every question in four minutes with perfect clarity
- the 81-year-old grandma who developed an app by coding everything herself

And then there's you.
Staring at a TypeError like it insulted your mother.

But here's what you don't see:

That genius teen didn't sleep for three days for the fifth time within a month.
That 12-line web server is unstable enough to cause WiFi outages.
That Advent of Code wizard has been doing it for a decade.
That StackOverflow legend no longer remembers what sunlight feels like.
That grandma is actually cool. Just saying.

Everyone struggles.
Nobody posts their struggles.

You only see the highlight reel.
Don't compare your backstage footage to someone else's movie trailer.

The Most Common Thoughts Developers Never Admit Out Loud

Let's normalize some very real inner monologues:

"I should probably know this by now."
No you shouldn't. The ecosystem is too big.

"Why does this bug feel personal?"
Because Python often makes it personal.

"Everyone else is progressing faster than me."
They're not. You see their successes, not their hours of staring at the ceiling.

"What if I'm not cut out for this?"
If you're thinking deeply about your path, you're exactly the kind of person who *is* cut out for this.

"My code is embarrassingly messy."
Great. So is everyone else's.
Clean code is not the default state of nature. Chaos is.

"If I ask a question, people will think I'm dumb."
Engineers love answering questions. It makes them feel wise and distracts them from their own chaos.

"I don't feel like a real developer."
The moment you said that and meant it, you became one.

What Real Confidence Actually Looks Like

Here's a secret:

Real confidence is not "I know everything."

Real confidence is:

"I don't know this yet, but I can figure it out."

That's it.

That's the entire skillset behind senior-level thinking.

Not memorizing.
Not perfection.
Not superhuman logic.

Just:

- curiosity
- patience
- the willingness to break things
- the humility to Google things
- and the resilience to keep going

Your Brain Is Just Tired, Not Incompetent

Half of impostor syndrome isn't lack of skill.
It's:

- too much caffeine
- too little caffeine
- bad sleep
- overwhelming documentation
- unclear error messages
- trying to learn concepts at the wrong time
- life stress
- hunger
- debugging fatigue
- trying something new at the end of a long day

You're not failing.
You're overloaded.

Brains aren't machines.
They don't respond well to being microwaved with constant new information.

Give yourself a break.

Literally.
Stand up.
Walk around.
Let your mental RAM clear.

Most "I'm stupid" moments disappear after a sandwich.

The Real Test of a Pythonista

Not whether you can write decorators.
Not whether async makes sense.
Not whether you know the difference between *args and **kwargs without Googling.

The real test is simple:

You came back after getting stuck.

That's it.

If you return to the keyboard after frustration, confusion, self-doubt, or a full emotional meltdown?

You're doing it right.

Programming isn't a straight upward climb.
It's a zig-zag of breakthroughs and breakdowns.

Every time you push a little further, you level up.
Quietly.
Invisibly.
Permanently.

You Are Not Alone And You Are Not a Fraud

If you've ever felt like you're tricking people into thinking you know what you're doing...

Guess what?

Everyone else feels the same way.

We're all wandering through the same maze, occasionally finding doorways, occasionally walking into walls.

The important part is that you're moving.

Impostor syndrome isn't proof that you're failing.
It's proof that you're growing.

You're stretching yourself.
You're trying something difficult.
You're learning skills most people never attempt.
You're improving more than you realize.

And every Pythonista, every single one, has been where you are.

The Warm Truth

Here's the comforting core of this chapter:

You belong in Python.
Not because you're flawless.
Not because you never get confused.
Not because everything comes naturally.

You belong because you're here.
Showing up.
Trying things.
Building things.
Breaking things.
Fixing things.

Laughing at error messages that feel like personal attacks. And getting a little better every time.

You are not an impostor.
You are a Pythonista in progress which is exactly what all of us are.

And you're doing great.

CHAPTER 16
The Zen of Python... Interpreted Honestly

There exists a mysterious poem hidden inside Python.
A philosophical guide.
A set of holy principles.

To access it, you type:

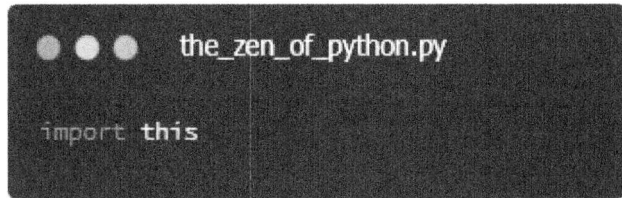

Python clears its throat, straightens its robe, and presents:

The Zen of Python

a collection of sayings written by Tim Peters, a man who
clearly understood both enlightenment and chaos.

The Zen of Python is beautiful.
It's wise.
It's also deeply hilarious when compared to the reality of
everyday coding.

So let's walk through each line... honestly.

1. Beautiful is better than ugly.

In theory:
Write clean, elegant code.

In practice:
You will write something beautiful...

then rewrite it at 2 AM into something that looks like a cryptic prophecy carved into a cave wall.

That's okay.
Beauty is subjective.
Especially when you're behind on a deadline.

2. Explicit is better than implicit.

Meaning:
Be clear. Be direct. Don't hide logic.

Reality:
You will absolutely write implicit code because you're tired and want to go home.
Then future-you will open the file, groan loudly, and say:

"Who did this?
...Oh no."

3. Simple is better than complex.

True.

Until your "simple" solution includes three decorators and a list comprehension that looks like a ransom note.

4. Complex is better than complicated.

This one is important:

- **Complex** = lots of parts, but understandable
- **Complicated** = a headache in code form

Most developers learn this difference around the time they break their first production environment.

5. Flat is better than nested.

This is Python's way of saying:

"Don't indent so much that your code disappears off the right side of the screen."

Beginners, however, nest code like they're building a Russian doll collection.

Veterans see four levels of indentation and immediately reach for coffee.

6. Sparse is better than dense.

We all agree with this.

Until we write a one-line list comprehension to impress someone.

Then suddenly we're okay with density levels approaching nuclear fusion.

7. Readability counts.

This is Python's core belief.

Readable code is good code.

However, readability drastically decreases with:

- lack of sleep
- emotional instability
- nested loops
- whoever wrote the code last
- functions named process_data_2

8. Special cases aren't special enough to break the rules.

Python says:
"Stick to the rules."

Developers say:
"I hear you... but what if I break the rules just this once?"

Spoiler:
We break the rules. Often.

And then blame Python when things explode.

9. Although practicality beats purity.

Translation:
"It's okay to do it the ugly way if the pretty way takes six hours and five brain cells you no longer have."

The Zen of Python is wise, but it also understands deadlines.

10. Errors should never pass silently.

Python throws bold, screaming red errors at you.
If you've read Chapter 4, you already know that's not anger.
That's affection. Very loud, very dramatic affection.

It doesn't let things slide.

It doesn't whisper, "Hey, something might be wrong."

It shouts:

"SOMETHING IS DEFINITELY WRONG AND I WILL NOT PROCEED UNTIL YOU FIX YOUR LIFE."

This line of Zen is Python saying:

"I'm doing this because I care."

11. Unless explicitly silenced.

Python:
"Don't silence errors."

Also Python:
"But if you really want to... okay."

Developers see this and write:

```python
try:
    do_the_thing()
except:
    pass
```

This is the coding equivalent of throwing a blanket over a fire and pretending the problem is gone.

12. In the face of ambiguity, refuse the temptation to guess.

Beginners guess constantly.

Intermediates guess with more confidence.

Veterans guess with spreadsheet-level analytics and still get it wrong.

Python wants clarity.
Developers want to finish the feature before lunch.

This is where the conflict lies.

13. There should be one — and preferably only one — obvious way to do it.

This is Python's polite roast of languages like Perl.

However, Python forgot its own rule and gave us:

- multiple ways to format strings
- multiple ways to import modules
- multiple ways to run async
- multiple ways to write loops
- multiple ways to open files

There is always one obvious way...
after you Google it.

14. Although that way may not be obvious at first unless you're Dutch.

This is Tim Peters joking about Guido van Rossum, Python's creator.

The real message?

"You're not supposed to get everything immediately."

Which, honestly, is comforting.

Especially when you're staring at decorators.

15. Now is better than never.

Developers interpret this as:

"Just fix it now."

Managers interpret this as:

"Just ship it now."

Both interpretations lead to therapy.

16. Although never is often better than *right now*.

This is the universe telling you:

"Don't deploy on Friday."

Ever.

17. If the implementation is hard to explain, it's a bad idea.

If you ever find yourself explaining your code with:

"So... this is a bit weird, but..."

Stop.

Start over.

Or at least write a comment apologizing to future-you.

18. If the implementation is easy to explain, it may be a good idea.

This is Python encouraging clarity.

If you can explain something in one sentence, it's probably safe.

Unless it's async.
Or classes.
Or decorators.
Or packaging.
Or anything, really.

Look, programming is complicated.
Do your best.

19. Namespaces are one honking great idea — let's do more of those!

This is Python celebrating organization.

Developers interpret it as:

"I didn't want these files together anyway."

Then we create:

- modules
- submodules
- packages
- **init** files
- folders inside folders
- and 15 python files named utils.py

Namespaces are great.
We just abuse them a little.

The Honest Takeaway

The Zen of Python is beautiful.
It's warm.
It's wise.

And it's aspirational like "eat more vegetables" or "stop checking your email after 6 PM."

You won't follow every principle perfectly.
Nobody does.

But knowing them shapes how you think:

- cleaner
- clearer
- simpler
- kinder to your future self

And that's the heart of Python.

Not perfection.
Not purity.

Just doing things in a way that makes life a little easier...
and a little less chaotic.

Even if your code still screams at you occasionally.

CHAPTER 17
Burnout and Breaks: Python Will Still Be Here When You Return

Burnout in programming doesn't arrive like a dramatic explosion.
It sneaks in quietly, disguised as "just one more bug," "just one more feature," or "just one more YouTube tutorial because I swear decorators will make sense eventually."

One minute you're coding happily.
The next minute you're staring at your screen like it personally betrayed you.

Burnout is universal.
Burnout is normal.
Burnout is survivable.

And Python, bless its chaotic heart, will wait for you.
It's not going anywhere.

Burnout Starts Subtly

It doesn't hit all at once.
It's a slow drip of little signs:

- rereading the same line of code eighteen times
- forgetting what function you're inside
- staring at the terminal until the terminal stares back
- typing a variable name wrong four times in a row
- Googling "why am I like this" instead of the actual error message

You tell yourself:

"I'm just tired. I'll push through."

This is the first lie developers tell themselves.

The second is:

"I'll go to sleep after this one last fix."

The third is:

"I can definitely finish this tonight."

No.
You can't.
And that's fine.

The Developer Burnout Cycle

Burnout has a predictable rhythm.
It goes something like this:

1. Enthusiasm Phase

"I love coding! I love Python! I love building things!"

You're unstoppable.
You're productive.
You watch tutorials for fun.
Your coffee tastes like victory.

2. Overcommitment Phase

"I can do that. Sure. And that. And also that."

Your task list grows like an invasive species.
You say yes to everything, because programming is just problem-solving and you like solving problems... until there are 46 of them.

3. The Slow Decline

You start noticing small signs:

- you stop cleaning your code
- your git commits start having messages like "ugh"
- you add TODOs you have no intention of doing
- your comments become emotional ("# why does this work??")

4. The Crash

Suddenly you're exhausted.

Your brain feels like someone stuffed it with wet bread.
You can't remember how for-loops work.
You open StackOverflow and the text blurs like an ancient prophecy.

Congratulations.
You've hit burnout.
Please fasten your seatbelt.

5. The Recovery

Eventually, you stop.
You rest.
And you remember:

"Oh. I'm a human being, not a code-generating machine."

This is progress.

6. The Return

You come back refreshed.
You write good code again.
You rediscover joy.

And then... slowly... the cycle begins anew.

But don't worry:
This time, you know the signs.

The Debugging Meltdown Moment

Every Pythonista hits a specific burnout point:

You're debugging something small.
Something simple.
Something trivial.

It doesn't work.

You flip to a different file.
That doesn't help.

You flip back.
Now you forget what you were doing.

You try a fix.
It fails.

You try another.
It explodes.

You hit that moment where you say:

"This should work,"
but your voice cracks like you're starring in an emotional drama.

This is the burnout tipping point.

Time to step away.

The Emotional Whiplash of Python

Python is funny.
Python is elegant.
Python is beautiful.

Python is also unpredictable, passive-aggressive, and deeply chaotic.

One day you're writing gorgeous list comprehensions.
The next day you're trying to remember how to open a file.

Burnout isn't caused by difficulty alone.
It's caused by the sudden swing between ease and frustration.

Your brain was not built for this rollercoaster.
Breaks aren't optional, they're maintenance.

Breaks Are Where Your Brain Reboots

Developers fear breaks because they think stopping means losing progress.

Not true.

Breaks are where half your real learning happens:

- your subconscious untangles the logic
- your brain connects patterns
- your memory consolidates
- your stress drains away
- your inner Pythonista reinflates like a balloon someone sat on

Ever notice how you leave a bug unsolved...
and when you return later the solution is suddenly obvious?

That's not magic.
That's cognitive defragmentation.

Your brain runs a background process called "Essential Developer Maintenance."
Let it run.

The Signs You Need a Break

If any of this feels familiar, step away immediately:

- You try to fix a bug by rewriting the entire project.
- You yell "WHY" at your computer like it owes you money.
- You're reading error messages in the voice of a disappointed parent.
- You forgot to eat lunch.
  Or breakfast.
  Or yesterday.
- You stared at the same function so long it feels like a personal enemy.
- The rubber duck is now judging you.

These are not challenges to push through.
These are alarm bells.

What Taking a Break Actually Looks Like

A break is not:

- checking email
- scrolling documentation
- watching YouTube tutorials
- researching a different bug
- opening a new project "for fun"

A break is:

- a walk
- a snack
- a nap
- a shower
- a conversation
- petting your dog
- staring into space like a Victorian poet contemplating mortality

Your brain is not a CPU.
It needs different fuel.

Python Will Still Be There When You Come Back

One of the most comforting truths in programming:

Code does not move on without you.

It doesn't grow mold.
It doesn't expire.
It doesn't mutate into something unrecognizable (unless a coworker touches it).
It doesn't run away because you took a day off.

Python is patient.

It will break at the same line of code tomorrow just as happily as it breaks today.

You can come back rested, refreshed, sane, hydrated.
And suddenly everything feels easier.

Python isn't testing you.
Your brain is just running low battery.

The Developer's Oath

Repeat after me:

"I will rest when I'm tired.
I will not debug during emotional distress.
I will remember that the bug is not personal.
I will hydrate.
I will eat something green occasionally.
I will not deploy on Fridays.
I will forgive myself for not knowing everything.
I will take breaks so I can keep coding tomorrow."

Burnout doesn't mean you're weak.
It means you're human.

And humans need rest.

You chose a demanding craft.
A messy craft.
A rewarding craft.

Take care of the person writing the code.
Not just the code itself.

CHAPTER 18
You're a Pythonista Now, Whether You Like It or Not

There comes a moment in every programmer's life when you stop asking:

"Am I a real Python developer?"

and start asking:

"Why does this cursed package only work on Python 3.9.7 with a waxing moon?"

This, my friend, is the moment of transformation.

Not graduation.
Not mastery.
Not enlightenment.

Acceptance.

You've crossed the invisible line.
You've survived installation issues, indentation trauma, debugging grief, dependency chaos, async nightmares, decorator witchcraft, and at least one emotional breakdown involving pip.

You didn't quit.

You didn't flee to another language.

You stayed.

Congratulations.

You are now a Pythonista, whether you like it or not.

You Didn't Notice the Moment It Happened

It wasn't dramatic.
No confetti.
No certificate.
No wise old programmer appearing to place a USB stick on your forehead and whisper, "It is time."

It sneaks up quietly.

One day, you realize you've been:

- reading error messages without panicking
- writing functions without staring at the keyboard
- Googling smarter
- using list comprehensions intentionally
- saying phrases like "it's probably a scoping issue"
- fixing bugs that terrified you a month ago
- and explaining something to a beginner... and sounding like you knew things

That's it.
That's the transformation.

You changed.
You leveled up without noticing.

Python Has Become Your Internal Monologue

A real Pythonista eventually starts thinking in code.

You see a list and think:

"map or list comprehension?"

You hear someone describe a problem and think:

"That's just a dictionary."

You hear the word "async" and instinctively wince.

You bump into indentation in the real world and feel a sharp pang of ancestral trauma.

Python has rewired part of your brain.
You're one of us now.

You Understand That Confusion Is Permanent

Beginners think confusion is temporary.

Real developers know:

Confusion is the natural resting state of programming.

You're not supposed to know everything.
You're not even supposed to know most things.

The Python ecosystem is huge.
The language keeps evolving.
Libraries multiply when you're not looking.

Being a Pythonista doesn't mean "I understand everything." It means:

"I understand enough to move forward, and I'm comfortable googling the rest."

That's the real badge of honor.

You've Built a Relationship With Python

It's not always healthy.
It's not always loving.
But it's a relationship.

You know Python's moods:

- When it's being friendly
- When it's being mysterious
- When it's being dramatic

- When it's punishing you for a missing parenthesis

You've seen Python at its best:

Readable.
Clean.
Helpful.
Elegant.

And you've seen Python at its worst:

When a tiny whitespace destroys your weekend.

You accept both sides.
This is love.
Or Stockholm syndrome.
Same difference.

You've Become Someone Beginners Look Up To

Even if you don't feel advanced, someone out there sees your work and thinks:

"Wow... I hope I can understand that one day."

And you will want to yell:

"No, don't look at me, I barely know what I'm doing."

But that's impostor syndrome talking.

The truth?

You *do* know things.
More than you think.
Enough to help someone else.
Enough to build something real.

You are part of the Python chain of wisdom now.
One link among many, pulling the next generation forward.

You Can Laugh at Your Past Self

Remember these moments?

Your first print()?
Your first SyntaxError?
Your first infinite loop that made your computer sound like a jet engine?
Your first time breaking pip so badly you considered changing identities?

You can laugh now.

Not because you've become perfect,
but because you've grown.

Every mistake taught you something.
Every frustration built resilience.
Every bug helped shape your instincts.

You are not the same person who wrote that first shaky script.

And you should be proud of that.

You've Earned This Title

You don't need permission.
You don't need a certificate.
You don't need a senior title on LinkedIn.
You don't need to pass a secret Python ritual (although solving a circular import should count as one).

If you write Python...
if you struggle with Python...
if you break Python...
if you fix Python...
if you come back after confusion, after errors, after burnout...

You're a Pythonista.

You're in the family now.

The Warmest Truth of All

At the end of the day, Python is not just a language.
It's a community.
A culture.
A shared madness.
A comfort.

And now, you're part of that world.

A world of:

- developers who care
- developers who help
- developers who laugh at their mistakes
- developers who write messy code at midnight
- developers who keep going

So take a moment.
Breathe.
Honor the journey.

You didn't accidentally stumble in.

You climbed your way here.
Bug by bug, line by line, coffee by coffee.

Welcome home.

You're a Pythonista now.

Whether you like it or not.

PART 5: BONUS
(Added under mild pressure from my editor)

BONUS CHAPTER 1
The Five Emotional Stages of a Failed Deployment

Deployments are the moments you discover who you truly are.
Not your strengths.
Not your resilience.
Your panic threshold.

Every Python programmer has lived through at least one deployment so catastrophic it felt like a character-building exercise forced upon them by the universe.

Welcome to the Five Emotional Stages of a Failed Deployment.
AKA the real Kübler-Ross model for developers.

Stage 1: Confidence (Delusion): "It worked locally."

This is the last moment of peace you will know.

You type:

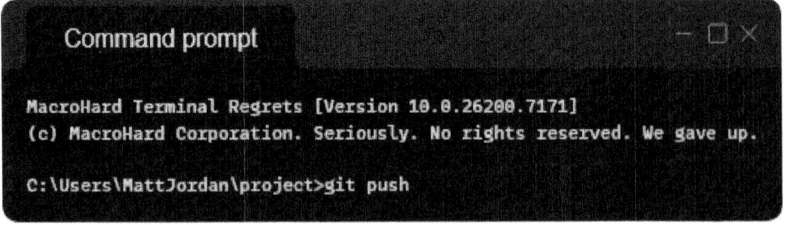

Or you click "Deploy" with the smugness of someone who believes they have defeated destiny itself.

You whisper:

"It's fine. Everything is fine."

The logs begin scrolling.
Your build server hums like a sleepy dragon.

You lean back in your chair, confident, calm...

...and entirely wrong.

"It worked locally" is the programming equivalent of "What's the worst that could happen?"

Never say it.
It summons demons.

Stage 2: Confusion: "Why... why isn't it working?"

Your deployment finishes.
You open the app.
It explodes instantly.

No warnings.
No logic.
Just pure, uncut chaos.

You refresh the page 12 times like a lab rat hitting a food button.

You mutter to yourself:

"But... it worked locally. It worked locally. IT WORKED LOCALLY."

Then you begin the sacred ritual:

The Developer's Panic Checklist

- Restart server
- Restart browser

- Restart self
- Clear cache
- Blame environment variables
- Blame the virtual environment
- Blame pip
- Blame past-you
- Blame future-you
- Blame everything except the code

This stage lasts anywhere from five minutes to the rest of your programming career.

Stage 3: Anger: "I HATE EVERYTHING ABOUT COMPUTERS."

Now you're in full meltdown.

You click things aggressively.
You type with unnecessary force.
Your coworkers slowly back away.

This is the moment when rational thought disappears, and your debugging style becomes feral:

- deleting random files
- reinstalling packages out of spite
- rewriting functions that weren't broken
- scrolling logs like you're trying to start a fire

You curse error messages personally.
They deserve it.

Especially the mocking ones:

```
Command prompt                              — □ ✕

MacroHard Terminal Regrets [Version 10.0.26200.7171]
(c) MacroHard Corporation. Seriously. No rights reserved. We gave up.

C:\Users\MattJordan\project>python completely_faultless_code.py
Traceback (most recent call last):
  File "C:\Users\MattJordan\project\completely_faultless_code.py",
  line 1, in <module>
    import something_that_definitely_exists
ModuleNotFoundError: No module named
'something_that_definitely_exists'
```

This is the stage where you begin saying things like:

"I swear if this doesn't work I'm switching careers."

You won't.
But you'll say it anyway.
Like Murtaugh softly proclaiming, "I'm too old for this shit."

Stage 4: Bargaining: "Please, please, I'll never code on Fridays again."

You're no longer debugging.
You are negotiating with fate.

You promise the universe:

- "I'll refactor properly if this works."
- "I won't ignore lint warnings ever again."
- "I'll finally fix that TODO I've been pretending not to see."
- "I'll test my code next time."
- "I'll stop hardcoding things. Probably."

You poke the logs like they might suddenly confess.

You add print statements out of desperation.

You rerun the deployment with tiny irrelevant changes, hoping Python will say,
"You know what? Fine."

This stage ends only when you finally discover the real cause of the problem.

It's always something humiliating.

Stage 5: Acceptance: "Oh, It was a typo!"

Every failed deployment ends with a moment of bitter, painful clarity.

You find the bug.

You stare at it.

You whisper:

"No."

But yes.

It was:

- a missing comma
- an unclosed quote
- the wrong environment variable
- a file path spelled incorrectly
- an import that points to the wrong module
- a config flag set to True instead of False
- or your personal favorite:
  you forgot to restart the server

You fix it.
You redeploy.
It works instantly.

You are relieved.
You are humbled.
You are emotionally damaged.

But you survived the deployment.

Again.

The Aftermath: The Post-Deployment Glow

Hours later, you're sitting quietly.

A coworker walks by.

"How did the deployment go?"

You answer calmly:

"Smooth."

Smooth.

The boldest lie a developer can tell.

But that's programming.

We struggle.
We panic.
We question everything.
We fix it.
We move on.

And next week?

We do it all over again.

BONUS CHAPTER 2
How to Read Code Written by Someone Who Hates You

Reading unfamiliar code is one of the purest forms of emotional adversity known to humankind.
It doesn't matter if the author is:

- a coworker
- a stranger
- your past self

...it always feels like the code was written by someone who had a personal vendetta against you.

This chapter is your survival manual.

Step 1: Denial: "This can't be the right file."

You open the code expecting clarity.

What you find is:

- 500+ lines in one function
- variable names like temp, data2, and x_xXFinal
- comments that contradict each other
- imports nobody uses
- logic that disappears and then reappears three pages later

You whisper:

"No, no, no... this must be the wrong file."

You check the name.
It's correct.

Your soul leaves your body.

Step 2: The Naming Horror Show

Variable names are windows into a developer's emotional state.
Unfortunately, some windows reveal crimes.

Examples you may encounter:

```
● ● ●              main.py

thing = 42
myListThing = []
obj = something()
re = some_regex()
final_final_REAL_final = compute()
```

You read them and think:

"These names tell a story. And the story is that the author gave up halfway through."

Worse are the "creative" names:

```
● ● ●                main.py

unicorn = 3
wobbly = True
angry_pickle = do_stuff()
```

You don't know what these variables represent.
You don't *want* to know.
You simply want to forget.

Step 3: Comments That Should Be Illegal

Bad code can be forgiven.
Bad comments cannot.

You will find comments like:

Spoiler:
They didn't.

Or the classic:

This is not comforting.

Or the deadly:

This comment is cursed.
Whoever touches that line will unleash the beast.

And the worst of all:

What logic?
Where?
Why?

This is not a comment.
This is a cry for serious mental help.

Step 4: The Architectural Crime Scene

You scroll.

And scroll.

And scroll.

The structure of the code begins to resemble:

- a maze
- a ransom note
- a fanfiction crossover between two incompatible programming paradigms

You find:

- nested if-statements 9 levels deep
- loops inside loops inside loops
- copy-pasted logic everywhere
- a global variable used 15 times because the developer was "in a hurry"

You want to scream at the author.

But you can't.

Because the author might be you.

Step 5: The Detective Phase

Eventually, you start piecing things together like a detective solving a murder.

You gather clues:

- Why is this function called three times?
- Why is this one never called?
- Why is this variable updated in only one specific scenario that never happens?

- Why is this exception silently swallowed like a dark secret?

You draw mental maps.
You take notes.
You stare intensely at your monitor as if it will confess under pressure.

At some point, you say:

"...I think I understand what it's trying to do."

This is progress.
False progress, but still, progress.

Step 6: Emotional Acceptance

You finally understand the code well enough to touch it.
You brace yourself.
You add a change.

It breaks.

Of course it breaks.

You undo your change.
You try something else.
It breaks again.

The code is not just bad.
It is vengeful.

But eventually, through patience, caffeine, and the silent hope that nobody asks who fixed it,
you tame the monster.

Step 7: The Final Revelation

You sit back.
You exhale.

You whisper bravely:

"I will rewrite this."

And then you don't.
Because deadlines exist.
You add three lines, fix the bug, and leave the rest untouched like an unexploded bomb.

That's the real wisdom of reading terrible code:

Fix the issue, not the universe.

Epilogue: The Ultimate Truth

Here's the twist:

You will one day open old code you wrote, code you remember writing proudly,
and you will think:

"Who wrote this garbage?
...Oh no."

You will experience:

- shame
- confusion
- disbelief
- and then acceptance

And you'll smile.

Because this is growth.

Bad code isn't proof of incompetence.
It's proof you've improved.

And reading code written by someone who hates you, whether that someone is a coworker or your past self, is just part of the journey.

You're stronger now.
You've survived.

Onward, Pythonista.

BONUS CHAPTER 3
The Pythonista's Field Guide to Annoying Bugs

Welcome, brave explorer.
Today you enter the wilderness of Python debugging: a harsh, unforgiving ecosystem filled with creatures that lurk silently in your code, waiting for the perfect moment to leap out and shout:

"HAHA, YOU MISSED A COMMA."

This field guide will help you identify the most notorious species you will encounter.
Study it well.
It may save your sanity.

1. The Heisenbug

Scientific name: *buggus disappears-when-observedus*

Description:
A mystical creature that vanishes instantly the moment you add a print() statement.

You see the bug.
You confirm the bug exists.
You attempt to catch it.
It disappears like a guilty toddler when their parent walks into the room.

You remove your debugging statements.
It returns.

Heisenbugs feed on your doubt.
They thrive on making you question your own memory.

Natural habitat:

- asynchronous code
- multithreading
- anything involving timing
- code you wrote while tired

Threat level:
High. Causes existential dread.

2. The Ghost ImportError

Scientific name: *importus randomly-failus*

Description:
This rare bug appears only when it's least convenient, usually while deploying or when demonstrating code to another human being.

Despite the module clearly existing in your project, despite installing it, reinstalling it, sacrificing a virtual environment to the gods, Python insists:

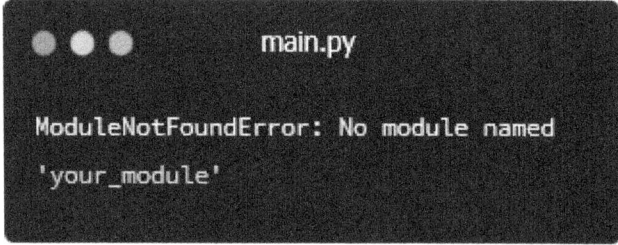

This bug is not logical.
This bug is emotional.

Behavior:

- appears only in one environment
- disappears after restarting
- reappears after you confidently say "It's fixed now"

Threat level:
Moderate. Causes spiritual confusion.

3. The Boolean Betrayer

Scientific name: *truthy falsy confusus*

Description:
A treacherous creature that looks innocent but stabs you when your guard is down.

You write:

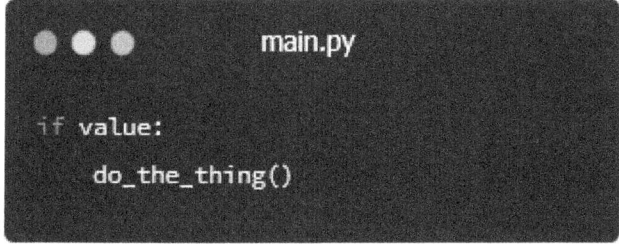

What counts as True?
What counts as False?
Why is an empty list considered False but a string with a single space is True?
Why do numbers pretend to be booleans when they feel like it?

The Boolean Betrayer enjoys watching developers debug for 45 minutes before discovering:

Or worse:

153

```
● ● ●          main.py

value = ""
```

Threat level:
Medium. Causes shouting at screens.

4. The Mutation Monster

Scientific name: *listus changes-when-you-didnt-askus*

Description:
This beast hides inside mutable data structures like lists and dictionaries.

Symptoms include:

- lists magically updating in multiple places
- dictionaries getting new keys you definitely did not add
- a function altering something you passed into it "for no reason"

The Mutation Monster thrives on shared references.
It grows stronger each time you forget that lists and dicts are mutable.

You think you created a copy.
You did not.

Now two entirely separate parts of your code are influencing each other like conjoined twins who share one terrible temper.

Threat level:
Severe. Causes deep trust issues.

5. The Off-by-One Gremlin

Scientific name: *indexus tragicus*

Description:
This creature is small but vicious.
Its favorite activity is destroying loops.

You expect a loop to run 10 times.
It runs 9.
Or 11.
Or it crashes with an IndexError that feels personal.

Even Python veterans are not immune.
You will fight the Off-by-One Gremlin your entire career.

Threat level:
Catastrophic. Causes premature aging.

6. The Zombie Bug

Scientific name: *fixus returns-from-the-deadus*

Description:
The Zombie Bug is a legendary creature known for disappearing after a fix and then mysteriously reappearing six weeks later in a completely unrelated part of the codebase.

You bury it.
You celebrate.
You brag.

Then one day:

"It's happening again."

Zombie Bugs never truly die.
They lie dormant, waiting for the right conditions, which is usually when your manager joins the Zoom call.

Threat level:
Very high. Causes PTSD.

7. The Circular Import Serpent

Scientific name: *snakus eats-its-own-tailus*

Description:
You import module A into module B.
Then you import module B into module A.
Python looks at you, sighs dramatically, and dies.

Circular imports are serpents devouring their own tail and your sanity.

The error messages are cryptic:

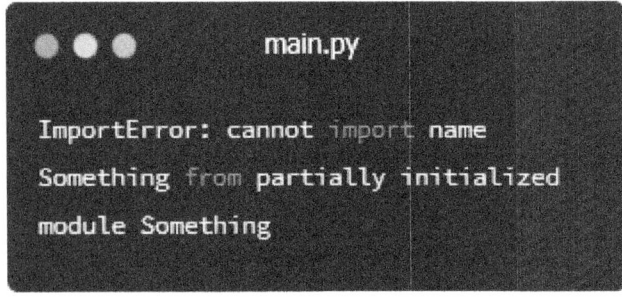

Translation:
"You summoned a demon. You know what you did."

Threat level:
Extreme. Causes pacing and deep philosophical questioning.

8. The "Works on My Machine" Phantom

Scientific name: *hauntus coworkerus*

Description:
This bug does not appear on your machine.
Only someone else's.

Your code runs flawlessly.
Your colleague runs it and:

- four errors appear
- nothing behaves normally
- the app crashes
- the logs scream

The Phantom lives between environments, thriving on minor differences:

- Python version
- package version
- OS
- timezone
- installed fonts
- sheer cosmic chaos

Threat level:
Unmeasurable. Causes finger-pointing and Slack messages.

9. The Silent Failure Shade

Scientific name: *except pass demonus*

Description:
This shadowy creature cares nothing for your sanity.

It hides inside try-except blocks like this:

```
● ● ●           main.py

try:
    risky_thing()
except:
    pass
```

Silent Failure Shades deliver:

- no logs
- no errors
- no hints
- just pain

You know something is wrong.
You see something is wrong.
But Python whispers, "All good :)" while everything burns behind the scenes.

Threat level:
Nuclear. Causes complete collapse of trust.

10. The Race Condition Raptor

Scientific name: *threadus velociraptor*

Description:
Rare but deadly.

Race conditions occur when two parts of your program try to access or change something at the same time.

The result?

- unpredictable errors
- inconsistent behavior
- the illusion of functionality
- intermittent chaos

A Race Condition Raptor is invisible until the moment everything collapses.

Threat level:
Terminal. Causes spontaneous screaming.

Final Advice for Surviving Bug Territory

If you encounter one of these creatures:

1. Stay calm.
2. Add print statements.
3. Remove print statements when they change the bug's behavior.
4. Google aggressively.
5. Take a walk.
6. Drink water.
7. Apologize to your rubber duck for yelling.
8. Fix the bug.
9. Forget how you fixed it.
10. Move on before something else breaks.

The wilderness of Python is wild but with a little patience, a lot of humor, and a few well-placed breakpoints, you'll survive.

BONUS CHAPTER 4
The StackOverflow Survival Guide

StackOverflow is the great temple of programming.
A sacred place where developers gather to seek wisdom, enlightenment, and the occasional emotional scolding.

It is beautiful.
It is terrifying.
It is absolutely necessary.

Every Pythonista must learn to navigate StackOverflow safely. This chapter is your guide through its jungles, pitfalls, and cryptic elders.

1. The First Rule: StackOverflow Is Faster Than Light

You post a question.

You hit "Submit."

You blink.

You already have:

- 2 comments
- 1 usable answer
- 1 edited title
- and one user asking you to "please add a minimal reproducible example"

All within four seconds.

StackOverflow's top answerers are not human.
They are either extremely caffeinated, omnipresent, or running personally optimized async event loops.

2. The Duplicate Police

If your question even resembles an existing question, StackOverflow will detect it with the precision of a military radar.

Immediately someone swoops in:

"This has been asked before."

Link provided.
Case closed.
Your self-esteem drops 15 points.

Welcome to StackOverflow.

To be fair...
sometimes the duplicate is from 2008, about Pascal, and only vaguely relevant.
But the duplicate police never sleep.

3. The Passive-Aggressive Commenter

You write your question.
You're vulnerable.
You're confused.
You need help.

Then someone comments:

"Have you considered reading the documentation?"

Translation:
"I am disappointed in you, but professionally."

Or worse:

"What exactly is your question?"

This is the StackOverflow version of
"Explain your feelings using bullet points."

4. The Answer That Is Technically Correct but Emotionally Devastating

Some answers solve your problem in one line.

But the explanation makes you feel like you've committed a war crime:

"You are clearly misunderstanding how Python handles mutable default arguments."

Or:

"This approach is obviously flawed."

Is it obvious?
Not to you.
Not to anyone you've ever met.
Not to your ancestors.

StackOverflow answers are less about clarity and more about establishing dominance.

5. The Ancient Sage Answer

Every once in a while, you find an answer from 12 years ago that:

- solves your exact problem
- is written in flawless simplicity
- contains wisdom so profound you question your own intelligence and existence

The author hasn't logged in since 2015.
Nobody knows where they are.
Some say they ascended.

This user is StackOverflow's equivalent of a mythological figure. A legend.

6. The Overkill Solution

Your problem is small:

"How do I merge two dictionaries?"

Someone answers:

"You could write a fully customizable dictionary-merging framework using metaclasses, descriptors, and a recursive generator."

They post 47 lines of code.
It works flawlessly.
It terrifies you.

StackOverflow teaches you there are always two solutions to every problem:

- the easy way
- the way someone with too much free time solved it

7. The One-Liner Wizard

This user answers your multi-paragraph question with:

"Just use sorted(set(nums), key=nums.index)."

No explanation.
No context.
Just black magic.

You try it.

It works.

You close your laptop, take a walk, and enjoy your newfound freedom.

8. Asking Your Own Question: The Developer Rite of Passage

Asking a StackOverflow question is emotionally harder than confessing your feelings to someone you like.

You must:

- write calmly
- supply reproducible code
- follow obscure formatting rules
- include environment details
- avoid sounding confused (even though you are)

Then you hit submit.

And instantly receive a comment saying:

"You have not provided enough information."

You cry softly.

This is normal.

9. When Someone Edits Your Question

A StackOverflow veteran edits your question for clarity.

You read the edited version and think:

"Wow... I wish I understood the problem that well."

Your original question was 60% panic, 20% rambling, 20% typos.

The edited version looks like a paragraph from a well-reviewed research paper that makes you question if you're good enough. Don't worry, you are.

Just be grateful.
You have just been blessed by a StackOverflow angel.

10. The Accepted Answer That You Don't Fully Understand

You click "Accept Answer."

You try the code.
It works.

You nod confidently while thinking:

"I have absolutely no idea why."

This is okay.

This is respectable.

This is tradition.

We have accepted answers we don't understand since the dawn of coding.

Final Advice for Surviving StackOverflow

Follow these spiritual guidelines:

- Be humble. Questions are welcomed. Panic is expected.
- Don't take the comments personally.
- Read the answers twice: once for logic, once for existential healing.
- Upvote the heroes who save you.
- Bookmark the answers you'll forget tomorrow.

- And remember: every expert you see once posted a question so embarrassing they deleted it immediately.

StackOverflow isn't just a website.

It's a rite of passage.
A digital monastery.
A communal therapy session disguised as Q&A.

And with enough time, practice, and a few dozen downvotes, you'll become part of its cycle too.

BONUS CHAPTER 5
Pythonisms You Pretend to Understand

Python is full of concepts you nod along to without really "getting."
You've heard them before.
You've used them in sentences.
You've even confidently explained them to beginners.

But deep down?

You were lying.

Don't worry.
We all do it.
This chapter is your safe space.

Let's explore the Python terms every developer pretends to understand while quietly Googling them at 1 AM.

1. Duck Typing

What experts say:
"Duck typing means that if it walks like a duck and quacks like a duck, it's a duck."

What beginners hear:
"Bring ducks."

What it actually means:
Python doesn't care what something *is*.
It only cares what it can do.

If it acts like the thing you need, Python shrugs and says, "Good enough."

Why nobody really understands it:
Because people keep explaining it using an actual barnyard animal.

Also, duck typing breaks dramatically when the object looks like a duck but throws a TypeError halfway through quacking.

2. First-Class Functions

What experts say:
"In Python, functions are first-class citizens."

What beginners think:
"Do we have second-class functions too?"

What it actually means:
You can treat functions like objects:

- pass them around
- store them in lists
- return them from other functions
- lose them accidentally
- question your life choices

Why nobody understands it:
Because humans aren't used to treating verbs like nouns.

3. Truthiness

What experts say:
"In Python, many values have truthiness."

What beginners think:
"Truthiness sounds like something a motivational speaker would sell."

What it actually means:
Python judges values morally.

- "" → False
- " " → True
- 0 → False
- 0.00001 → True
- [] → False
- [None] → True
- "False" → True (and emotionally confusing)

Everything has an opinion about whether it counts as "true."

Why nobody understands it:
Because Python's emotional criteria for truth is unpredictable and personal.

4. Context Managers

What experts say:
"Use a context manager to handle setup and teardown automatically."

What beginners hear:
"Use... a manager... to manage the context?"

What it actually means:
When you write:

```
● ● ●                main.py

with open("file.txt") as f:
    data = f.read()
```

Python handles:

- opening
- closing

- cleaning
- sadness
- cleanup from sadness

Context managers are the adults in the room who clean up after your mess.

Why nobody understands it:
Because everyone knows with open()...
but nobody remembers how to write their own context manager without Googling the tutorial with the coffee example.

5. Decorators

You already know this one is witchcraft.

We covered it before, but let's be honest:

Nobody truly understands decorators except the five monks who live in a mountain and maintain Python's core.

Everyone else:

- copies them
- pastes them
- prays they work
- pretends they fully grasp the weird nested functions
- blames async when they don't

Why nobody understands it:
Because decorators are recursive code origami.

6. Generators vs Iterators

What experts say:
"A generator is an iterator but not all iterators are generators."

Amazing.

Thank you for clarifying absolutely nothing.

Generators are functions that return one item at a time using yield.

Iterators are objects that can return one item at a time using __next__().

That's the whole difference.

Why nobody understands it:
Because yield behaves like a mysterious form of time travel that pauses the universe.

Generators feel like:

- "return... but gentle"
- "return... but again"
- "return... but in installments, like a payment plan"

7. Descriptors

What experts say:
Descriptors power Python's attribute access protocol.

What beginners hear:
"Ahhhhhhhhhh."

What it actually means:
...

Nobody really knows.

Descriptors are the kind of advanced feature you only learn about while reading an article titled:
"Why Is My Property Acting Weird?"

Why nobody understands it:
Because descriptors were created by and for framework

authors and extremely bored geniuses. Not by and for normal, functioning humans.

8. Metaclasses

The crown jewel of confusion.

What experts say:
"A metaclass is a class that creates classes."

What beginners hear:
"Python is sentient?"

Metaclasses are Python's highest-level magic.
They let you change how classes behave at creation time.

Which sounds cool until you actually see metaclass code and feel your consciousness detach from your physical body.

Why nobody understands it:
Because metaclasses are like:

- decorators' evil grandparents
- inheritance on caffeine
- classes that write other classes at compile time
- a feature used by ORMs, frameworks, and nobody else, ever

Every Pythonista has Googled:

Q   python metaclass simple explanation   ✕   ⟳ AI Mode

None of the explanations were simple.

9. The GIL (Global Interpreter Lock)

What experts say:
"The GIL ensures that only one thread executes Python bytecode at a time."

What beginners hear:
"Python doesn't do multithreading... unless it does?"

What it actually means:
Python protects itself from chaos by saying:

"One at a time, please."

It's like having a fast-food restaurant with 10 employees but only one register.

Why nobody understands it:
Because it's the reason Python threads are weird...
but also the reason Python memory is stable...
but also the reason performance memes exist...
and everything is confusing.

10. The Walrus Operator: :=

Introduced in Python 3.8 and instantly misunderstood by everyone.

What experts say:
"It assigns values inside expressions!"

What beginners think:
"Why does Python have emoji now?"

Why nobody understands it:
Nobody asked for it.
Nobody uses it right.

Everyone feels slightly guilty when they do.

Final Wisdom: Nobody Actually Understands Everything

Here's the warm truth:

The Python ecosystem is huge and weird and full of brilliant features you absolutely do not need to master to be a real Pythonista.

You can live a long, happy coding life without ever touching:

- metaclasses
- descriptors
- context managers you wrote yourself
- duck typing theory
- generator pipelines
- custom decorators
- the GIL
- the walrus operator
- anything involving time zones

Python was not designed for omniscience.
It was designed for survival.

You're doing great if your code:

- runs
- mostly works
- doesn't catch on fire
- is understandable by your future self 40% of the time

Pythonisms are confusing for everyone but the fact that you're learning them, laughing at them, and using them anyway?

That's what makes you a real Pythonista.

A Note From Matt

(Don't you hate people who refer to themselves in third person?)

Hey.
You made it all the way to the end. That says something about you.

Not that you're stubborn or caffeine-powered or quietly losing your mind over a missing parenthesis.
Although... it might say that too.

Mostly, it says this:

You kept going.

You pushed through installation disasters, indentation trauma, async nightmares, decorator witchcraft, and bugs that simply should not exist according to the known laws of the universe.
And you're still here; curious, trying, learning, moving forward.

That's what makes you a real Pythonista.

Not knowing everything.
Not writing perfect code.
Not remembering how virtual environments work (which is normal; that knowledge evaporates every 48 hours).

Being a Pythonista means:

showing up
trying again
laughing when it works
laughing harder when it doesn't
taking breaks before you emotionally combust
coming back anyway

If you take nothing else from this book, take this:

You're doing better than you think.

And you're a lot closer than you realize.

Keep learning.
Keep experimenting.
Build weird things.
Break them.
Fix them.
Be proud of all of it.

And when Python inevitably screams at you again, remember:
you're not alone. You're part of a big, slightly chaotic, deeply
supportive tribe of people who also wonder why their code
works only on Tuesdays.

I'm cheering for you.
And I'm genuinely proud of you for getting this far.

See you out there, Pythonista.
If you ever feel lost, just flip back to Chapter 1 and remind
yourself:
you've already beaten the first boss fight.

You have, and are surviving, being a programmer.
Keep it up.

Matt Jordan

About the Author

(Because apparently you're supposed to know who wrote the thing you just read.)

Matt Jordan is a Python educator, humor enthusiast, and the accidental founder of the "Python Beginners Who Are Trying Their Best" support group (membership: everyone interested).

He has been writing Python long enough to know that indentation will betray you, pip will break your environment at the worst possible moment, and that print()-based debugging is not a flaw, it's a lifestyle choice he refuses to apologize for.

Matt is the man behind ZeroToPyHero, where he writes just about all the articles himself, mostly because he has far too many thoughts about Python, insists on putting them somewhere, and cares maybe a bit too much of the mental healthcare of all Pythonistas. His work focuses on helping beginners learn the language without losing their confidence, sanity, or sense of humor, and make seasoned Pythonistas laugh a bit.

When he's not writing or teaching, Matt can usually be found:

- wrestling with virtual environments
- insisting he'll "clean up the code later"
- drinking coffee strong enough to qualify as a personality trait
- reminding new programmers that yes, they really can do this

Matt believes Python should feel approachable, human, a little chaotic, and occasionally hilarious, much like the people who choose to learn it.

He's proud of you for making it through this book.
He hopes you're proud of yourself, too.

Printed in Dunstable, United Kingdom